# Women's Study Bible

# Also from EATMS Productions

Books on power, survival, women's autonomy, and the systems shaping modern America.

## Nonfiction

### Billionaires, Capitalism, and Power

Evil and the Mountain Ungreed
Self Help for American Billionaires
Selfish Steve and the Ivory Tower
Tariffs, Taxes, & Face-Eating Leopards
Ban Billionaires: Fascism Fix

### Fascism, Religion, and Cultural Control

Self Help for the Manosphere
Fascism 2025
Fascism & the Perverts & the Greed Virus
Christian Fascism Marriage Book
Tyranny, Table Manners, & Tiramisu

### Guides for Women's Autonomy and Protection

How to Survive in Post-America as a Woman
Project 2025 American Drag
4B – Burn, Ban, Boycott, Build
4B OG – So No Go GYN
I'm Glad He's Dead

### Analysis of Authoritarian Project 2025

Project 2025: The Blueprint
Project 2025: The List
Project 2025, Christian Dumb Dumbs, & The Republican Agenda
Fascism, Project 2025, & The Pinkprint

Modern Rewrites for Women

Stoic Principles Reimagined
Siddhartha Reimagined
The Prince Reimagined for Women
The Art of War Reimagined for Women
The Jungle Reimagined
The Constitution Reimagined for Women

Machine Learning Series

AI, Bitcoin, Nostr for Women
AI, Safety, & Security for Women
AI, Anxiety, & Health for Women
AI, Kids, & Family Safety for Women
AI, Creativity, & Personal Expression for Women
AI, Independent Work, & Parallel Power for Women

Social Systems Series

Emotional Labor for Women
Household Power for Women
Workplace Power for Women
Medical Bias for Women
Aging Systems for Women
Recovery Systems for Women

# Fiction

Dystopian Stories of Resistance and Collapse

Propaganda Paige & the Missing Prosperity
Propaganda Paige & the TIDE Manifesto
Propaganda Paige & the Shadow Cartographers
Propaganda Paige & the Prosperity Alliance
Propaganda Paige & the Shattered Truth
Propaganda Paige & the Rising TIDE
Propaganda Paige & the Last Bastion
Propaganda Paige & the Dawn of Prosperity
Project 2025: Dorian — The Last Men
Project 2025: Boy — A Last Men Novel

# Project 2025
# Women's Study Bible

F*ck the patriarchy 2

by
Esme Mees
& Petra Nein

EATMS
PRODUCTIONS

ISBN 979-8-9909279-3-3

Cover, interior design, interior prints by: Esme Mees

www.eatms.me
eatms@pm.me

Printed in the United States of America.

# Table of Contents

# Introduction
## *Women's Study Bible FTP*

Welcome to American Drag (Part 1)

Patriarchy is nothing more than an elaborate drag performance, one
that has dominated the world stage for millennia. It is a constructed
spectacle, carefully choreographed to obscure its origins and maintain
its illusion of inevitability. Just as drag reveals the artifice of gender
roles through subversion, exaggeration, and creativity, this book aims
to peel back the layers of patriarchal power to expose the seams of its
costume. But unlike drag, which celebrates fluidity and challenges
constraints, patriarchy demands rigid adherence to roles it has
fabricated, branding them as natural, divine, and immutable. It
dresses itself in the language of morality, biology, and religion,
ensuring its performance is mistaken for reality. This is the first
illusion we must dismantle: the belief that patriarchal power is
anything but an elaborate act.

To understand patriarchy as a performance is to recognize its
dependence on repetition and societal complicity. Every institution,
from the family to the church, from education to government, serves
as a stage upon which this performance unfolds. Patriarchy relies on
scripts handed down through generations, directing women to submit,
men to dominate, and everyone to accept these roles as unchanging
truths. These roles are not chosen freely but enforced, with those who
deviate punished or ostracized. This performance is not spontaneous;
it is deliberate, rehearsed, and maintained through fear,
manipulation, and coercion.

Consider the doctrine of "natural order," a favorite prop in
patriarchy's drag routine. It claims that men are naturally suited for
leadership, strength, and rationality, while women are biologically
inclined toward submission, emotion, and care. This narrative,
repeated ad nauseam, serves as a foundation for countless laws,
customs, and religious teachings that perpetuate inequality. Yet when
we examine history, biology, or scripture with a critical eye, this so-
called natural order unravels. History is replete with women who led,
fought, and created against all odds, and biology reveals no inherent

intellectual or emotional superiority between genders. Even scripture, which has been used to bolster patriarchal claims, offers moments of radical disruption that challenge these norms. The "natural order" is nothing more than a lie, told often enough to be mistaken for truth.

Patriarchy's performance does not end with its false claims of inevitability; it extends to its supposed divine mandate. Religion, perhaps more than any other institution, has been co-opted as patriarchy's stage manager. Sacred texts are edited, translated, and interpreted through a patriarchal lens, ensuring that their liberatory messages are obscured and their oppressive interpretations amplified. Eve is not remembered as the first seeker of knowledge but as the first sinner. Mary Magdalene, a leader in the early Christian movement, is reduced to a penitent sinner. These distortions are not accidents; they are deliberate acts of erasure and misrepresentation, ensuring that women are denied agency and power within their spiritual traditions.

The façade of divinity is perhaps patriarchy's most insidious costume. It uses religion not only to enforce gender roles but also to stifle liberation. How can one question the laws of men if they are presented as the laws of God? This conflation of patriarchal authority with divine will creates a nearly unassailable defense, one that has silenced countless voices of dissent. Yet even within this oppressive framework, cracks appear. The Bible itself contains stories of liberation and liberation, from Miriam leading the Israelites in song to Jesus defying social norms to uplift women. These moments remind us that the sacred is not inherently patriarchal; it has been made so through centuries of manipulation. Reclaiming these texts is not an act of blasphemy but of faith, a refusal to allow the divine to be weaponized against the oppressed.

To see patriarchy as performance is to understand that its power lies not in its inevitability but in its ability to control the narrative. This narrative is reinforced through cultural norms, legal systems, and economic structures, all of which work together to sustain the illusion. Take, for example, the family structure, long heralded as the cornerstone of civilization. Patriarchy's ideal family, a male breadwinner, a submissive wife, obedient children, is presented as both universal and timeless. Yet this model is neither. It is a relatively recent invention, shaped by industrial capitalism and colonialism, designed to consolidate male power and control over property, labor, and reproduction. By framing this structure as God-given, patriarchy ensures that its economic exploitation and gendered division of labor are seen as moral imperatives rather than systems of oppression.

The same can be said of political power. Patriarchal systems rely on hierarchies, presenting male dominance as the natural order of governance. Whether in monarchies, democracies, or dictatorships, the underlying assumption has long been that men are better suited to lead. This belief is reinforced not by evidence but by exclusion, ensuring that women and marginalized genders are denied access to power and, therefore, the opportunity to challenge the status quo. The few exceptions, queens, revolutionaries, or elected leaders, are often framed as anomalies, exceptions that prove the rule. Yet their very existence exposes the lie of patriarchy's inevitability, reminding us that power is not a birthright but a construct.

The performative nature of patriarchy also reveals itself in its fragility. Like any performance, it requires constant effort to maintain. It must suppress dissent, rewrite history, and punish deviation to preserve its illusion of authority. This is why liberation, even in its smallest forms, is so threatening to patriarchal systems. A woman refusing to conform to traditional roles, a community reinterpreting scripture, a movement challenging the status quo, these acts expose the cracks in patriarchy's façade, revealing it as the construct it is. Liberation is not only possible but inevitable, for no performance can last forever.

By understanding patriarchy as a drag performance, we reclaim the power to disrupt and dismantle it. This is not a call to mimic its methods but to subvert them, to use creativity, solidarity, and critical engagement to expose its artifice and build something new. Just as drag celebrates the fluidity and possibility of identity, so too can we imagine a world where power is not defined by domination but by collaboration, not by exclusion but by inclusion. The first step is to see patriarchy for what it is: a poorly scripted play whose time has come to an end. The curtain is lifting, and the stage is ours.


Welcome to American Drag (Part 2)

To understand the stakes of this work, we must first situate it within the political climate of Project 2025, a moment in history marked by an authoritarian resurgence, cultural regression, and the systematic erosion of civil liberties. This regime is not content to merely halt progress; it seeks to reverse it, dismantling the fragile gains made by feminist movements, civil rights advocates, and marginalized communities over decades of struggle. Its agenda is bold in its cruelty and unapologetic in its ambition: to consolidate power by co-opting religion, weaponizing tradition, and silencing dissent. For women, the implications are particularly dire, as the regime wages an all-out assault on reproductive rights, economic autonomy, and bodily agency. This is the backdrop against which we write, a world teetering on the edge of a patriarchal revival disguised as moral clarity and national restoration.

The blueprint for Project 2025 is both chilling and familiar, echoing the strategies of past authoritarian regimes. It seeks to blur the lines between church and state, using religious rhetoric to justify policies that entrench inequality and stifle opposition. By wrapping its agenda in the language of faith and family, it obscures its true aim: the consolidation of power in the hands of the few at the expense of the many. Women, as historical targets of both religious and political control, are among the first casualties of this agenda. Through laws restricting access to healthcare, dismantling workplace protections, and criminalizing dissent, the regime seeks to relegate women to roles of subservience and silence. Yet this is not simply a war against women; it is a war against democracy, equality, and the very idea of human dignity.

To challenge this regime, we must first understand its strategy. Project 2025 thrives on the co-optation of sacred texts, twisting them to serve its patriarchal and authoritarian goals. It relies on selective interpretations of scripture, emphasizing obedience, submission, and hierarchy while erasing the radical calls for justice, liberation, and love that also permeate these texts. This is a deliberate act of manipulation, designed to cloak oppression in the guise of divine will. By doing so, the regime not only justifies its actions but also discourages liberation, framing dissent as heresy and rebellion as sin. This weaponization of faith is one of the regime's most powerful tools, for it attacks not only the body but also the soul, undermining the spiritual and moral foundations of those it seeks to subjugate.

Liberation, therefore, requires more than political action; it demands a reclaiming of the spiritual and moral narratives that have been co-opted by power. This book offers a framework for such liberation, rooted in critical engagement with sacred texts. It is not enough to reject the patriarchal interpretations of scripture; we must actively challenge and subvert them, reclaiming these texts as tools for liberation rather than chains. This is an act of intellectual and spiritual defiance, one that requires courage, creativity, and a willingness to confront uncomfortable truths about the ways in which religion has been used as a tool of oppression.

The methodology we propose is threefold: deconstruction, reclamation, and reconstruction. Deconstruction is the first step, an unflinching examination of the ways in which sacred texts have been distorted to serve patriarchal and authoritarian agendas. This involves exposing the historical and cultural contexts of these distortions, revealing the ways in which they have been shaped by human agendas rather than divine intent. Take, for example, the oft-cited Pauline directive that "women should remain silent in the churches" (1 Corinthians 14:34). This verse has been used for centuries to silence women in religious spaces, but a closer examination reveals its context: a patriarchal society in which women's voices were seen as disruptive to the established order. By understanding this context, we can strip the verse of its oppressive power, revealing it as a reflection of cultural norms rather than a divine command.

Reclamation follows deconstruction, and it is here that we begin to wield scripture as a tool for liberation. This involves rediscovering the liberatory messages within sacred texts, amplifying the voices of those who have been marginalized or erased. Figures like Mary Magdalene, often maligned or diminished in traditional interpretations, emerge as powerful symbols of liberation and agency. Stories of liberation, from the Exodus to the resurrection, become blueprints for collective action and spiritual empowerment. This reclamation is not about cherry-picking verses to fit a progressive agenda; it is about uncovering the deeper truths within scripture, truths that challenge the hierarchies and oppressions imposed by patriarchal systems.

Finally, reconstruction involves building something new from the foundations of what we have deconstructed and reclaimed. It is not enough to critique and reclaim; we must also reimagine and create.

This involves reinterpreting scripture in ways that affirm the dignity and worth of all people, emphasizing themes of justice, love, and liberation. It also involves creating new rituals, practices, and communities that reflect these values, providing spaces for healing, empowerment, and liberation. This is not an act of rejection but of transformation, a refusal to allow sacred texts to be monopolized by those who seek to oppress.

This framework is not a mere intellectual exercise; it is a call to action. In the face of Project 2025 and the resurgence of authoritarian patriarchy, we cannot afford to remain passive. Liberation requires active engagement, a willingness to challenge the narratives that sustain oppression and to offer alternatives that inspire hope and courage. This book is both a guide and a companion in that struggle, offering tools for deconstruction, reclamation, and reconstruction that can be applied in personal, communal, and societal contexts.

At its core, this framework is about reclaiming power, spiritual, intellectual, and political, from those who seek to hoard it. It is about rejecting the false binaries that divide the sacred from the secular, the spiritual from the political, and recognizing that true liberation requires the integration of all aspects of our lives. It is about understanding that faith, when reclaimed and reimagined, can be a source of strength and solidarity in the fight against oppression. This is the promise of American Drag: to expose the performance of patriarchy, to reclaim the narratives it has stolen, and to build a world in which justice, equality, and love prevail.

As we move forward, let us remember that liberation is not a solitary act but a collective effort. It is forged in solidarity, sustained by dialogue, and driven by an unwavering commitment to justice. The political climate of Project 2025 may seem overwhelming, but history has shown that even the most entrenched systems of oppression can be dismantled through collective action and sustained liberation. This book is a testament to that truth, a reminder that the tools of our liberation are within our grasp if we have the courage to use them. Together, we can drag the patriarchy into the light, exposing its performance for what it is and reclaiming the power it has stolen. The stage is set, and the revolution begins now.

# FTP Proclamation

This book's mission is as bold as it is necessary: to reclaim scripture as a source of liberation rather than oppression and to turn the tide against the patriarchal forces that have co-opted the sacred for their own ends. For too long, religious texts have been used as tools to subjugate, silence, and control, their liberatory potential buried under centuries of dogma and distortion. But scripture is not inherently patriarchal; it is not a monolith of control. It is a living, breathing testament to the complexities of human experience, full of contradictions, tensions, and possibilities. The time has come to resist the narrow interpretations that bind and to reinterpret these texts as sources of empowerment and justice. This is not just an intellectual exercise but a spiritual and political act of defiance. To reclaim scripture is to reclaim the right to define ourselves, to tell our own stories, and to dismantle the systems that seek to dictate our roles, our bodies, and our destinies.

This mission demands nothing less than a radical reimagining of the role scripture plays in our lives and our societies. It begins with rejecting the lies we have been told about the inevitability of patriarchal theology. The notion that God has ordained hierarchy, that faith requires submission to human authorities cloaked in divine approval, is a fabrication designed to consolidate power. It is a lie told by those who fear the transformative power of equality and justice. Scripture, when stripped of these distortions, reveals something entirely different: a call to liberation, a demand for justice, and a vision of a world where the oppressed are lifted, and the powerful are humbled.

To resist patriarchal theology is to engage in a battle over meaning itself. The words of scripture are not static; they are interpreted, reinterpreted, and weaponized by those who seek to control their narrative. Patriarchy thrives on its ability to monopolize these interpretations, to claim exclusive rights to the divine voice. But interpretation is not the sole property of the powerful; it is the right and responsibility of all who seek truth and justice. This book is a call to reclaim that right, to wrest scripture from the hands of those who would use it to oppress and to wield it instead as a weapon of liberation. In this act of reclamation lies the potential to dismantle the very foundations of patriarchal power.

Reclaiming scripture is also an act of pragmatism. Power belongs to those who understand and wield it effectively. Scripture, for better or worse, is a source of immense cultural and spiritual power. It shapes laws, norms, and identities; it influences politics and personal decisions alike. To ignore its role is to cede this power to those who will use it to perpetuate injustice. To engage with it critically, to reinterpret and reclaim it, is to take back control of one of the most potent tools in human history. This is not about winning theological debates; it is about challenging the narratives that sustain oppression and offering alternatives that inspire resistance and change.

This pragmatic engagement with scripture is deeply connected to the broader struggle for decolonization. Just as colonial powers sought to erase the identities and histories of the colonized, patriarchal systems have sought to erase the identities and histories of women and other marginalized groups within religious traditions. To reclaim scripture is to reclaim identity, to restore the narratives that have been silenced and to assert the right to define ourselves on our own terms. It is an act of decolonization, a refusal to accept the roles and labels imposed upon us by those who fear our power.

Decolonization is not merely an academic concept; it is a lived and ongoing process. It requires us to confront the ways in which we have internalized the logic of colonization and patriarchy, to unlearn the narratives that have been used to control us, and to create new narratives that reflect our truths. Scripture, when reclaimed, becomes a tool in this process. It offers stories of resistance and resilience, of individuals and communities defying the odds and challenging the powers that be. These stories, reinterpreted through the lens of liberation, can inspire and guide us as we navigate the complexities of our own struggles.

This reclamation and reinterpretation of scripture are not acts of isolation; they are acts of solidarity. They connect us to the generations of women and marginalized people who have resisted oppression, often at great personal cost. They remind us that we are not alone in this struggle, that we stand on the shoulders of those who have come before us, and that our efforts will pave the way for those who come after. This is the power of scripture: it is not only a tool of resistance but also a source of connection, a reminder that our struggles are part of a larger story of liberation.

The call to action is clear: join this movement of resistance and reinterpretation, a movement that combines spiritual empowerment with radical defiance of oppressive systems. This is a movement that refuses to accept the false dichotomy between faith and freedom, between spirituality and resistance. It is a movement that recognizes the power of scripture to inspire, to challenge, and to transform. It is a movement that invites you to take up the tools of critical engagement and to use them to dismantle the structures that seek to control and define us.

Let this be a proclamation of defiance and hope. Let it be a reminder that power lies not in submission but in the courage to question, to challenge, and to change. Let it be a call to reclaim what has been stolen, to reinterpret what has been distorted, and to rebuild what has been broken. Together, we can transform scripture from a tool of oppression into a source of liberation, a foundation for a world where justice and equality prevail. This is the mission of *American Drag*, and it begins with you.

This is also an *American Drag* in every sense of the phrase. What a drag it is for this nation, now mired in the regressive quagmire of Project 2025, to be shackled by policies that strip away the hard-won freedoms and civil liberties that once defined its promise. What a drag for America to find itself on the world stage, not as a beacon of progress or a champion of democracy, but as a cautionary tale of how quickly rights can be eroded under the guise of moral restoration. This is the ultimate American drag: a land that prided itself on liberty and justice for all, now dragged down by authoritarian dogma, patriarchal oppression, and the relentless grind of policies designed to serve the few at the expense of the many. But drag also reveals, and this is where the drag of America's current state becomes its potential salvation. By confronting this weight, exposing the lies, and reclaiming the ideals that have been perverted, we can transform this drag into a movement, a revolutionary act of subversion, resistance, and liberation that reimagines what America can and must be.

Drag is also the act of inhaling a cigarette or hot smoke, a deliberate draw that fills the lungs with something heavy, sharp, and often toxic.

# Part I
*Deconstructing Patriarchy in Scripture*

Overview

The story of patriarchy's dominance cannot be told without examining its deep and calculated entanglement with religious texts. Across centuries, patriarchal systems have meticulously crafted a narrative that presents inequality not as a social construct but as a divinely ordained truth. These systems have relied on the authority of sacred scripture to solidify their power, using selective interpretations to justify oppression and frame dissent as heresy. Religious texts, originally meant to guide, inspire, and challenge humanity, have instead been weaponized to enforce hierarchies that marginalize women and perpetuate injustice. This weaponization is not incidental, it is an intentional strategy, an act of power cloaked in the language of faith. Understanding this manipulation is the first step toward dismantling it.

At the heart of this strategy is a simple but devastating sleight of hand: the reduction of complex, multi-faceted texts into tools of control. Patriarchy thrives on simplicity because simplicity leaves no room for questions, complexity, or dissent. Consider the story of Eve, which has been used as a cornerstone for the theology of female subjugation. Stripped of its richness, this narrative has been reduced to a cautionary tale against women's autonomy, framing Eve as the source of humanity's downfall. Yet a closer reading reveals something far more profound. Eve's choice to eat from the Tree of Knowledge is not an act of defiance against divine will but a courageous pursuit of understanding. Her story is one of agency, a moment of human complexity and choice. That her narrative has been distorted into a warning against women's independence is not a failure of the text but a deliberate act of patriarchal erasure.

The consequences of these distortions are staggering. Religious texts have been used to justify laws, shape cultural norms, and define individual identities, embedding inequality into the very fabric of society. Women have been confined to the domestic sphere, their voices silenced in public and spiritual spaces. In many religious traditions, the roles available to women are limited to those of obedience and service, often under the guise of divine mandate. This institutionalized inequality is not merely a product of historical context; it is an active and ongoing tool of control. Patriarchy's grip on scripture has ensured that its interpretation serves the powerful, creating a theology that not only justifies oppression but demands it.

This manipulation extends beyond gender, intersecting with systems of race, class, and colonialism to create a web of oppression that touches every aspect of life. The same interpretive strategies that silence women are used to marginalize entire communities, framing poverty, suffering, and disenfranchisement as natural or deserved. Religious institutions have often been complicit in these systems, using their moral authority to legitimize violence and inequality. But to blame scripture itself is to misunderstand the problem. The issue lies not in the texts but in the interpretive lenses through which they have been read, lenses ground and polished by centuries of patriarchal and colonial agendas.

Reclaiming scripture begins with recognizing its complexity. These texts are not monolithic; they are dynamic, contradictory, and profoundly human. They contain moments of oppression and liberation, injustice and justice, despair and hope. The task of deconstructing patriarchy in scripture is not about discarding these texts but about engaging with them critically and courageously. It is about peeling back the layers of distortion to uncover the truths that have been buried, to find the voices that have been silenced, and to reclaim the liberatory potential that lies within.

The story of Miriam offers a striking example. Often overshadowed by her brother Moses, Miriam plays a crucial role in the Exodus narrative, leading the Israelites in song and dance after their liberation from Egypt. Yet her contributions are frequently minimized or ignored in traditional interpretations, her leadership dismissed as secondary to Moses' divine mission. This erasure is not accidental; it is a reflection of patriarchal priorities that prioritize male leadership and diminish women's roles. Reclaiming Miriam's story means recognizing her as a leader in her own right, a figure of resilience and faith whose voice is as vital to the narrative as any man's.

The urgency of this work cannot be overstated. In the current political climate, movements like Project 2025 seek to weaponize religious rhetoric to roll back progress and entrench systems of oppression. These movements thrive on the manipulation of scripture, using it to justify policies that harm women, LGBTQ+ individuals, and marginalized communities. To leave these texts unchallenged is to cede ground to those who would use them as tools of domination. Reclaiming scripture is not just a theological exercise; it is an act of resistance, a refusal to allow the sacred to be used as a weapon against the vulnerable.

Reclamation also requires us to confront the ways in which we have internalized patriarchal interpretations of scripture. For many, these narratives are not merely external forces but deeply ingrained beliefs that shape our understanding of ourselves and our place in the world. Challenging these beliefs is painful and uncomfortable, but it is also liberating. It requires us to ask difficult questions: Who benefits from this interpretation? Whose voices are being silenced? What truths have been hidden, and why? These questions are not just academic; they are personal and political, touching every aspect of our lives.

The work of deconstructing patriarchy in scripture is also profoundly hopeful. It is a reminder that the sacred is not static but alive, capable of growth, change, and transformation. Scripture, when read critically and with an eye toward justice, can become a source of empowerment rather than oppression. It can inspire resistance, build solidarity, and ignite the imagination. The very texts that have been used to harm can be reclaimed as tools for healing and liberation. This is the promise of reclaiming scripture: not to erase its complexities but to embrace them, to find in its contradictions a mirror of our own struggles and triumphs.

This section begins that work. It is an invitation to engage with scripture not as a passive recipient but as an active participant, to challenge the narratives that have been imposed upon us and to create new ones that reflect our values and experiences. It is an act of faith in the transformative power of the sacred, a belief that these texts, when freed from the chains of patriarchy, can become instruments of justice and love. In a world that seeks to divide and oppress, reclaiming scripture is an act of defiance, a declaration that the sacred belongs to all of us. This work is not easy, but it is necessary, and its time is now.

Genesis as Ground Zero

The book of Genesis, the opening text of the Judeo-Christian Bible, is where it all begins, both for the narrative of creation and for the roots of patriarchal ideology that have shaped millennia of religious and cultural norms. It is, in many ways, ground zero for the theological justification of gender inequality, a foundational text that has been interpreted and wielded to establish and perpetuate male dominance. Yet, as with so much of scripture, the story Genesis tells is far more complex, nuanced, and contradictory than the interpretations imposed upon it by centuries of patriarchal authority. To understand how this text became a cornerstone of patriarchal ideology, we must first peel back the layers of interpretation to examine the text itself, its historical context, and the ways it has been used, and misused, in service of power.

At the heart of Genesis is the creation narrative, a story that has been endlessly retold, reframed, and politicized. The opening chapters of Genesis present two accounts of creation, often referred to as the Priestly account (Genesis 1:1–2:3) and the Yahwist account (Genesis 2:4–3:24). The first account, with its poetic cadence and cosmic scope, speaks of a God who creates humanity, male and female, in the divine image. "So God created humankind in his image, in the image of God he created them; male and female he created them" (Genesis 1:27). Here, humanity is presented as equal and united, both male and female bearing the divine imprint. This vision is one of profound equality, with no indication of hierarchy or subordination between genders.

Yet it is the second account, the Yahwist narrative, that has become the focal point for patriarchal interpretation. In this version, humanity begins with the creation of Adam, a lone man fashioned from the dust of the earth. Eve is introduced later, formed from Adam's rib to serve as his "helper" (Genesis 2:18–22). This sequence of events has been read for centuries as evidence of women's secondary and subordinate status, a reading that says far more about the priorities of its interpreters than it does about the text itself. The Hebrew term often translated as "helper" (ezer) does not imply inferiority; in fact, it is frequently used elsewhere in the Bible to describe God's role as a helper to humanity. Nonetheless, patriarchal interpreters have seized upon this word and the sequence of creation to construct a narrative of female dependence and male primacy.

The story of the Fall, recounted in Genesis 3, has done even more to solidify Genesis as ground zero for patriarchal theology. In this narrative, Eve is tempted by the serpent to eat from the Tree of Knowledge of Good and Evil, an act that leads to humanity's expulsion from Eden. Traditional interpretations have framed Eve as the primary transgressor, her actions seen as the origin of sin and suffering in the world. This reading has been used to justify the subjugation of women, portraying them as morally weak, easily deceived, and in need of male guidance and control. Yet this interpretation is neither inevitable nor universal. A closer reading of the text reveals a story of human complexity, curiosity, and agency, qualities that patriarchal systems have long sought to suppress, particularly in women.

Eve's decision to eat the fruit is often portrayed as a moment of defiance, but it is also an act of profound courage and autonomy. She chooses to seek knowledge, to question the boundaries imposed upon her, and to take a step into the unknown. This is not the act of a weak or foolish individual but of a fully human being wrestling with the complexities of choice and consequence. Adam, too, eats the fruit, yet his actions are rarely subjected to the same scrutiny or condemnation as Eve's. This double standard is a reflection not of the text but of the patriarchal lens through which it has been read, a lens that seeks to place blame on women while excusing or minimizing the actions of men.

The consequences of the Fall are often framed as a divine punishment, a curse that establishes the natural order of male dominance and female subordination. "Your desire shall be for your husband, and he shall rule over you," God tells Eve in Genesis 3:16. Yet this passage, like so much of Genesis, has been shaped and reshaped by interpretation. Is this statement a prescriptive command, endorsing male dominance, or a descriptive lament, acknowledging the reality of a broken and unjust world? The latter reading aligns more closely with the broader themes of scripture, which consistently call for justice, equality, and the restoration of right relationships.

The patriarchal interpretation of Genesis has not gone unchallenged. Feminist theologians and scholars have long pointed out the ways in which these readings distort the text and obscure its more liberatory possibilities. For example, the fact that both Adam and Eve are expelled from Eden and share equally in the consequences of their actions suggests a shared humanity and accountability that transcends gender. Similarly, the presence of two distinct creation narratives, one emphasizing equality and the other hierarchy, invites readers to wrestle with the tensions and contradictions within the text rather than accepting a single, monolithic interpretation.

Genesis has also been reclaimed as a source of empowerment and resistance. Eve, once vilified as the archetype of sin, can be reimagined as a symbol of agency and the pursuit of knowledge. The creation of humanity in the divine image, male and female alike, serves as a powerful affirmation of gender equality. These alternative readings do not deny the text's complexity or its capacity for harm, but they offer a way to engage with it critically and creatively, transforming it into a tool for liberation rather than oppression.

The importance of this work cannot be overstated. Genesis is not merely a story about the beginning of the world; it is a story about the beginning of interpretation, the foundational narrative upon which entire systems of belief and power have been built. To challenge the patriarchal interpretations of Genesis is to challenge the very foundations of those systems, to dismantle the ideologies that have used scripture as a weapon against women and marginalized groups. It is to reclaim the text as a living, dynamic source of meaning, one that can inspire justice, equality, and the pursuit of truth.

Genesis, as ground zero for patriarchal theology, is also ground zero for its deconstruction. By peeling back the layers of distortion, by reading the text with fresh eyes and open hearts, we can begin to uncover its deeper truths and possibilities. This work is not about erasing the past but about reimagining the future, about creating a world in which scripture is no longer a tool of oppression but a source of liberation and hope. This is the promise of Genesis, and it is a promise worth reclaiming.

Genesis Reloaded - Eve as the First Rebel
Traditional Readings of Eve

Eve, the first woman of the Judeo-Christian narrative, has long borne
the weight of a story that frames her as the archetypal sinner, the
origin of humanity's fall from grace. Traditional interpretations have
cast her as the weak link in creation, a figure of moral failure whose
actions unleashed a cascade of suffering and estrangement from God.
This portrayal, while pervasive, is not a neutral or inevitable reading
of the text but a deliberate construct that has served patriarchal
agendas for centuries. By positioning Eve as the root of sin, these
interpretations have justified the subjugation of women, framing them
as inherently flawed, untrustworthy, and in need of male control.

The traditional reading of Genesis 3, often referred to as "The Fall,"
hinges on Eve's encounter with the serpent and her decision to eat
from the Tree of Knowledge of Good and Evil. The serpent, often
interpreted as a manifestation of temptation or evil, approaches Eve
with a question that challenges the boundary God has set: "Did God
really say, 'You must not eat from any tree in the garden'?" (Genesis
3:1). In response, Eve engages in dialogue, clarifying the command
and showing her awareness of the divine restriction. However, the
serpent's persuasive rhetoric leads her to reconsider, and she chooses
to eat the fruit and share it with Adam. This moment has been
interpreted as a moral failure, a woman succumbing to deception,
dragging humanity into sin.

From this narrative, centuries of theological discourse have
extrapolated a sweeping indictment of women's character and role in
society. Eve's act has been framed as emblematic of women's
supposed susceptibility to deception, their emotional instability, and
their dangerous independence. Church fathers like Augustine and
Tertullian took this narrative and wove it into theological frameworks
that painted women as the gateway to sin. Tertullian, in his infamous
condemnation, referred to women as "the devil's gateway," blaming
Eve's actions for humanity's suffering and loss of paradise. This
interpretation not only stigmatized women but also justified their
exclusion from leadership, education, and autonomy within religious
and societal structures.

The consequences of this framing are far-reaching. Eve's portrayal as the first sinner has been used to justify centuries of systemic inequality, from barring women from clergy roles to dictating their behavior and dress. Her supposed failure has been wielded as a cautionary tale to enforce obedience, silence, and submission. In this reading, Eve becomes the prototype of every woman's guilt—a figure whose actions define the limits of female agency and whose punishment (pain in childbirth and subordination to her husband) is eternalized as divinely ordained justice.

Yet, even within the traditional reading, contradictions emerge. If Eve's actions are seen as the origin of sin, why is Adam's complicity often overlooked or minimized? Adam, after all, accepts the fruit without question and eats it, yet he is not subjected to the same moral scrutiny or blame. This double standard reflects the patriarchal lens through which the story has been interpreted, a lens that seeks to place the burden of sin squarely on Eve, excusing or Adam's role.

The traditional reading also raises deeper questions about the nature of sin, choice, and consequence. If Eve's actions were the result of deception, does that absolve her of full accountability? If she was acting out of curiosity or a desire for knowledge, does that make her inherently sinful, or does it reveal something profoundly human? These questions point to the limitations of the traditional interpretation, which reduces a complex narrative to a simplistic morality tale designed to control and condemn.

The framing of Eve as the archetypal sinner is a reflection of the priorities and biases of those who have interpreted it. By reducing Eve to a symbol of failure, traditional readings have obscured the richness and complexity of her story, turning a narrative about humanity's struggle with choice and consequence into a justification for gendered oppression. This reductive interpretation has shaped not only theology but also cultural and social norms, leaving a legacy of harm.

Understanding the construction of Eve's narrative as the archetypal sinner is crucial to reclaiming her story and challenging the systems of oppression it has supported. It is the first step in peeling back the layers of distortion to uncover the deeper truths and possibilities within the text, truths that reveal Eve not as a figure of failure but as a symbol of agency, courage, and humanity's quest for knowledge.

Patriarchy's Use of the Narrative

The patriarchal framing of Eve as the archetypal sinner is one of the most enduring and harmful narratives in the history of religious interpretation. By reducing her story to an act of failure and disobedience, patriarchy has used this portrayal to justify the systemic subjugation of women, perpetuating stereotypes that cast them as inherently untrustworthy, morally weak, and dangerous when independent. This narrative has not only shaped theology but also underpinned social, cultural, and legal structures, embedding gender inequality into the fabric of societies for centuries.

At the core of this patriarchal use of the narrative is the idea that Eve, by succumbing to temptation, embodies the supposed flaws of all women. Her actions in the Garden of Eden have been weaponized to construct a theology that views women as the weaker sex, more prone to error, less capable of leadership, and in need of male guidance and control. The consequences of this framing are vast. In religious contexts, it has been used to bar women from positions of authority, to silence their voices in places of worship, and to relegate them to roles of servitude. Women's spiritual contributions have been undervalued or dismissed entirely, their humanity overshadowed by a narrative that paints them as perpetual penitents, forever bearing the guilt of original sin.

This theological justification for subjugation extends far beyond religious institutions. By presenting Eve's disobedience as emblematic of female nature, patriarchy has established a foundation for societal norms that confine women to the domestic sphere and enforce rigid gender roles. Women are expected to be passive, obedient, and deferential, reflecting the supposed lesson of Eve's punishment: that a woman's primary function is to serve and support, not to lead or question. These expectations have shaped laws and customs, from property rights that historically placed women under the control of their fathers or husbands to educational barriers that denied women access to knowledge and independence.

The harmful stereotypes perpetuated by this narrative are pervasive and insidious. The idea that women are emotionally unstable, easily deceived, or inherently untrustworthy has fueled discrimination and violence against them. In workplaces, women are often subjected to higher standards of scrutiny or excluded from decision-making roles, their competence doubted because of lingering cultural biases rooted in this ancient story. In relationships, the stereotype of women as manipulative or morally frail has justified controlling behavior and abuse, reinforcing cycles of domination and oppression.

Perhaps the most devastating aspect of patriarchy's use of this narrative is the way it has been internalized by women themselves. The constant repetition of Eve's story as a cautionary tale has instilled feelings of guilt, shame, and inferiority in countless women. Many are taught to view their ambitions, desires, or autonomy as dangerous, echoing the warnings embedded in the narrative of the Fall. This internalized oppression manifests in self-doubt, diminished aspirations, and an acceptance of unequal treatment as ordained.

The selective focus on Eve's role in the Fall also serves to erase or downplay the complicity of men in both the biblical story and the systems of power it has inspired. Adam, who willingly eats the fruit offered by Eve, is rarely scrutinized to the same degree. Instead, his role is often reframed as a passive mistake, a momentary lapse of judgment, while Eve's actions are elevated to a symbol of all human downfall. This double standard reinforces the patriarchal narrative that men are natural leaders and women are natural liabilities.

Patriarchy's use of the Eve narrative has also been instrumental in perpetuating sexual control over women. By framing Eve's sin as the origin of human suffering, her body and her desires become sites of suspicion and regulation. Female sexuality is cast as dangerous, something to be controlled by male authority to prevent further moral or social corruption. This framing has justified practices ranging from chastity vows and purity culture to the policing of women's bodies through dress codes, reproductive restrictions, and outright violence.

To challenge the patriarchy's use of this narrative, it is essential to reclaim Eve's story and reinterpret it through a lens of liberation and equality. Rather than accepting her as a symbol of failure, we can view her as a figure of agency and curiosity, a human being navigating the complexities of choice and consequence. By confronting the stereotypes and structures rooted in the patriarchal reading of Genesis, we begin to dismantle the systems of control that have oppressed women for centuries.

Reclaiming Eve's Agency

Eve's story, long twisted into a cautionary tale of disobedience and failure, is ripe for reclamation as a narrative of agency, curiosity, and the pursuit of knowledge. Far from being the archetypal sinner, Eve can and should be seen as the first rebel, a figure who refuses to accept unquestioned boundaries and dares to seek understanding even at great personal cost. This reinterpretation does not ignore the consequences of her actions but reframes them as the result of a conscious and courageous choice. In reclaiming Eve's agency, we challenge the patriarchal norms that have used her story to justify female subjugation and affirm the right of all people, particularly women, to think, question, and act independently.

At the heart of this reinterpretation is Eve's encounter with the serpent and her decision to eat the fruit from the Tree of Knowledge of Good and Evil. The traditional narrative frames this act as an unthinking lapse, a failure to adhere to divine command. Yet the text itself paints a different picture. Eve does not eat the fruit impulsively; she deliberates. She observes that the tree is "good for food and pleasing to the eye, and also desirable for gaining wisdom" (Genesis 3:6). Her actions are thoughtful, motivated by a desire for knowledge and growth rather than rebellion for rebellion's sake. This is not the behavior of a foolish or morally weak individual but of a human being seeking understanding, a pursuit that is, arguably, a reflection of the divine image in which she was created.

In this light, Eve's actions challenge the boundaries imposed upon her. She questions the prohibition placed on the tree, engaging in dialogue with the serpent and considering the implications of her choice. This willingness to interrogate authority is itself an act of agency, one that defies the patriarchal expectation of blind obedience. Eve's decision to eat the fruit is not a failure; it is a moment of profound human courage. It reflects the complexities of free will, the tensions between obedience and autonomy, and the inherent risks of seeking knowledge. In choosing to eat the fruit, Eve steps into the unknown, embracing the possibility of transformation even as she faces the certainty of consequences.

Reinterpreting Eve as a seeker of knowledge disrupts the patriarchal framing that has long positioned women as passive, dependent, and incapable of independent thought. Her story becomes a testament to the power of curiosity and the necessity of questioning the status quo. It is a reminder that progress, spiritual, intellectual, or otherwise, is often born of discomfort and risk. By reclaiming Eve's agency, we also reclaim the right of all people, particularly women, to engage with the complexities of faith and life without fear of condemnation.

Eve's act of seeking knowledge also serves as a powerful counter-narrative to the patriarchal ideal of submission. Patriarchy thrives on the suppression of questions, the enforcement of boundaries, and the denial of agency. It demands that women, in particular, conform to roles of obedience and silence, accepting the limitations imposed upon them without challenge. Eve's story, reinterpreted, becomes a direct challenge to this demand. It asserts that the pursuit of knowledge, even when it disrupts established norms, is not a sin but a virtue. It affirms that agency and autonomy are inherent to the human experience and that these qualities are not the exclusive domain of men.

This reclaimed narrative also invites us to reconsider the consequences of Eve's choice. The expulsion from Eden, often seen as a punishment, can be reimagined as a necessary step in humanity's journey toward growth and self-awareness. By eating the fruit, Eve initiates a transition from innocence to experience, from dependence to maturity. This transition is painful, but it is also transformative. It mirrors the struggles inherent in human existence, the tension between safety and freedom, between comfort and growth. In this reading, Eve is not the cause of humanity's downfall but the catalyst for its evolution.

Reclaiming Eve as the first rebel is not about ignoring the pain and complexity of her story but about recognizing the strength and humanity within it. Her narrative, long used to justify oppression, becomes a source of inspiration and empowerment. It reminds us that questioning authority, seeking knowledge, and embracing agency are not acts of defiance but acts of faith, faith in our capacity to grow, to learn, and to transform the world around us. This reinterpretation of Eve challenges the patriarchal systems that have sought to control women's bodies, minds, and spirits for centuries. It affirms that women are not passive recipients of divine will but active participants in the unfolding story of creation.

Broader Implications

Reclaiming Eve's narrative as a story of agency, courage, and the pursuit of knowledge has profound implications that extend far beyond Genesis. It disrupts the patriarchal lens through which not only the creation story but much of the Bible has been interpreted, challenging deeply entrenched readings that prioritize male authority and diminish women's roles. By reframing Eve as a figure of empowerment rather than transgression, we unlock new possibilities for understanding other biblical texts, breaking the stranglehold of interpretations that reinforce gender inequality and opening the door to liberatory readings that affirm dignity, agency, and equality for all.

The traditional framing of Eve as the archetypal sinner has long been used to justify the subordination of women, casting them as weak, morally suspect, and in need of male oversight. This interpretation has shaped readings of other biblical women, positioning them within a framework of passivity and dependence. Figures like Mary Magdalene, the Samaritan woman at the well, and even the Virgin Mary have been read through this lens, their narratives often stripped of their complexity and agency. Reclaiming Eve's story disrupts this pattern, providing a foundation for reimagining the roles of women in scripture as active, dynamic participants in God's work.

For example, consider the story of Sarah and Hagar in Genesis, a narrative often read as a tale of male authority and divine will enacted through Abraham. Reclaiming Eve's agency encourages us to look beyond Abraham's actions and explore the complex, intersecting lives of Sarah and Hagar. Sarah, too often reduced to the role of a barren wife desperate for a child, can be seen as a woman navigating societal pressures and her own limitations. Hagar, often framed as a victim of Sarah and Abraham's decisions, emerges as a figure of resilience, encountering God directly in her moment of greatest need. Reclaiming Eve's narrative invites us to view these women not as footnotes to a patriarchal story but as central figures with voices, struggles, and agency.

Similarly, the reinterpretation of Eve disrupts the traditional readings of Mary Magdalene, whose story has been overshadowed by centuries of mischaracterization as a repentant sinner. The patriarchal impulse to cast Mary Magdalene in a subordinate, morally tainted role mirrors the distortions imposed on Eve. Yet Mary Magdalene, like Eve, is a seeker of truth, a witness to the resurrection, and a leader within the early Christian community. Reclaiming Eve's courage and agency helps us see Mary Magdalene not as a figure of shame but as a revolutionary voice in the Gospel narrative, challenging societal norms and bearing witness to transformative truth.

Beyond individual stories, reclaiming Eve's narrative challenges broader theological constructs that have been used to subordinate women. Traditional interpretations of passages like 1 Corinthians 14:34-35, where Paul writes that women should remain silent in church, rely on the premise of female inferiority rooted in the Eve narrative. By reframing Eve's story as one of agency and strength, we undermine the theological foundations of such arguments, revealing them as products of cultural bias rather than divine intent. This shift enables us to approach these texts with fresh eyes, uncovering their historical contexts and exposing the ways in which they have been manipulated to sustain patriarchal systems.

The ripple effects of reclaiming Eve extend to contemporary issues of gender justice, offering a framework for confronting the ways in which religious narratives continue to shape societal norms. By disrupting patriarchal readings of scripture, we challenge the exclusion of women from leadership, the policing of women's bodies, and the silencing of women's voices in spiritual and secular spaces. Reclaiming Eve's story empowers women to see themselves not as subjects of divine punishment but as co-creators in the ongoing work of justice, liberation, and transformation.

Ultimately, reclaiming Eve's narrative disrupts the notion that scripture is inherently patriarchal, revealing instead its potential to inspire resistance and affirm the inherent worth of all people. This work is not simply about rewriting one story but about dismantling the entire framework that has been used to oppress, replacing it with a vision of equality, mutuality, and shared humanity.

The Proverbs 31 Myth - Virtuous, Not Subjugated Introduction to
Proverbs 31

The 31st chapter of Proverbs has long been held up as the
quintessential portrait of the "ideal woman," a guidepost for female
virtue that has been preached, memorized, and inscribed on countless
church programs, devotional journals, and household decorations.
Titled "The Wife of Noble Character" in many translations, this
passage has become a cultural touchstone for conservative and
patriarchal notions of womanhood, revered as a timeless blueprint for
what women should aspire to be. The Proverbs 31 woman is
celebrated for her industriousness, her dedication to her family, her
resourcefulness, and her faith. Yet, beneath the surface of this
veneration lies a troubling dynamic: the ways in which this passage
has been co-opted to enforce rigid, restrictive gender roles and
perpetuate a narrow, subjugating vision of femininity.

Proverbs 31 has been weaponized by patriarchal systems to confine
women within specific roles, primarily as wives, mothers, and
homemakers. It has been used to valorize unpaid labor in the home,
to prioritize domestic submission over public leadership, and to place
the burden of spiritual and familial success squarely on women's
shoulders. Women are told to emulate this ideal, but the version of the
Proverbs 31 woman they are presented with is often a distorted one,
filtered through the lens of cultural expectations that have little to do
with the text itself. Stripped of its historical and literary context, this
chapter becomes a checklist for unattainable perfection, setting
women up for a lifetime of striving and shame.

The cultural fixation on Proverbs 31 as a blueprint for womanhood
reveals as much about those who promote it as it does about the text
itself. The passage is often cherry-picked to emphasize qualities that
align with patriarchal ideals, submission, caregiving, and self-sacrifice,
while ignoring the broader picture of the woman described. In many
interpretations, the Proverbs 31 woman is framed as a servant to her
husband and children, her value measured by how well she upholds
the home and fulfills others' needs. This narrow framing not only
diminishes her complexity but also erases the independence, strength,
and entrepreneurial spirit she demonstrates in the text.

What is often overlooked in popular readings is that Proverbs 31 describes a woman who is far more dynamic and multifaceted than the caricature presented in many sermons and devotionals. She is a savvy businesswoman, engaging in trade and managing her own enterprises. She is a leader in her community, providing for the poor and making decisions that benefit those beyond her household. She embodies strength and dignity, speaking with wisdom and acting with confidence. These qualities—agency, intellect, and independence—are rarely emphasized in patriarchal interpretations, which instead reduce the passage to a manual for subservience and domestic labor.

This reductionist approach not only misrepresents the Proverbs 31 woman but also places an unrealistic and oppressive burden on women in contemporary society. The expectation to embody every virtue described in the passage, to be simultaneously a tireless homemaker, a successful entrepreneur, a devoted wife, and a compassionate community leader, is not just unattainable but harmful. It reinforces the idea that women's worth is tied to their ability to meet impossible standards, often at the expense of their well-being and autonomy. For many women, the Proverbs 31 ideal becomes a source of guilt and inadequacy rather than inspiration.

Understanding how Proverbs 31 has been co-opted as a tool of patriarchal control is essential to reclaiming its deeper meaning. The chapter, when read critically and in context, offers a vision of womanhood that is powerful, independent, and resourceful, qualities that challenge rather than uphold the constraints of traditional gender roles. By peeling back the layers of distortion and examining the text on its own terms, we can begin to liberate the Proverbs 31 woman from the shackles of cultural expectation and reveal her as a figure of strength and empowerment.

Patriarchal Misuse

The patriarchal misuse of Proverbs 31 has transformed what could be
a celebration of women's strength and resourcefulness into a tool for
confining them to restrictive and outdated domestic roles. This
chapter, often titled "The Wife of Noble Character," has been
repeatedly cherry-picked and stripped of its historical and literary
context, reducing a vibrant and multifaceted figure into little more
than a servant of her family. By presenting Proverbs 31 as an
unyielding standard for women to emulate, patriarchal systems have
weaponized the text to reinforce traditional gender hierarchies, limit
women's autonomy, and place the burden of familial and societal
success squarely on their shoulders.

At the heart of this misuse is the selective emphasis on domesticity. In
countless sermons, devotionals, and teachings, the Proverbs 31
woman is framed as the quintessential homemaker, rising early to
prepare meals, ensuring her household runs smoothly, and caring
tirelessly for her family. While these elements are present in the text,
they are highlighted to the exclusion of her other qualities, such as her
entrepreneurial acumen, leadership, and strength. This selective
reading creates a narrow ideal, one that prioritizes a woman's role
within the home above all else and dismisses her contributions outside
of it. The result is a caricature of womanhood, one that serves
patriarchal interests by limiting women's roles to caregiving and
domestic labor.

This weaponization of Proverbs 31 has profound consequences. By
presenting the chapter as a divinely ordained standard, patriarchal
systems place immense pressure on women to conform to roles that
may not align with their gifts, aspirations, or circumstances. Women
are told that their value lies in their ability to serve others, primarily
their husbands and children, rather than in their own intrinsic worth
or achievements. This message not only stifles women's ambitions but
also creates a sense of guilt and inadequacy when they fail to meet the
impossible expectations laid out for them. For single women, childless
women, or those who pursue careers outside the home, the Proverbs
31 ideal becomes a source of alienation, a reminder that they do not
fit into the mold of "godly womanhood" as defined by patriarchal
culture.

What is often ignored in these interpretations is the full scope of the Proverbs 31 woman's activities. The text describes a woman who is deeply engaged in commerce, purchasing land, planting vineyards, and trading goods. She is a decision-maker, a provider, and a leader who commands respect in her community. These aspects of the passage are often downplayed or recast in ways that diminish their significance, suggesting that her entrepreneurial efforts are merely an extension of her domestic duties rather than expressions of independence and skill. This reframing ensures that women are not inspired to see themselves as leaders or innovators but are instead encouraged to focus solely on their responsibilities within the home.

Moreover, the patriarchal emphasis on the Proverbs 31 woman's subservience to her husband is a distortion of the text. While the passage acknowledges her relationship with her husband, it does so in a way that highlights mutual respect rather than subjugation. The text states that her husband trusts her and praises her, a far cry from the hierarchical model promoted by patriarchal readings. By recasting her as a submissive figure, patriarchal interpreters erase the balance and partnership evident in the text, reinforcing a model of male dominance that the passage does not inherently endorse.

This misuse of Proverbs 31 also serves to maintain broader systems of inequality. By confining women to domestic roles, patriarchal interpretations ensure that men remain unchallenged in positions of power within religious, professional, and societal spheres. The glorification of women's unpaid labor within the home reinforces economic disparities and limits opportunities for women to engage in leadership or activism. It is a system that benefits from women's silence, sacrifice, and service, all while framing these constraints as virtues to be celebrated.

To reclaim Proverbs 31 is to expose these distortions and reveal the text's broader message of empowerment. The woman described in this chapter is not a symbol of submission but a figure of strength, wisdom, and resourcefulness. Her life is not confined to the home but extends into the community, the marketplace, and beyond. By restoring this context, we can liberate Proverbs 31 from its patriarchal chains and celebrate it as a testament to women's agency and leadership rather than a manual for their subjugation.

Liberating Proverbs 31

The Proverbs 31 woman, often held up as a symbol of domestic virtue, is far more dynamic and entrepreneurial than traditional interpretations suggest. When the text is examined closely and freed from the confines of patriarchal distortion, it becomes clear that she is a powerful figure of independence, resourcefulness, and leadership. Her contributions extend well beyond the home, challenging the narrative that confines her to domestic roles and offering a broader, more liberating vision of womanhood.

Proverbs 31 depicts a woman deeply engaged in economic and community life. She is described as a shrewd entrepreneur, a landowner, and a trader. "She considers a field and buys it; out of her earnings, she plants a vineyard" (Proverbs 31:16). This is not a passive figure content to operate within narrowly defined boundaries. Instead, she actively assesses opportunities, invests wisely, and cultivates resources that sustain her family and contribute to her community. The act of purchasing land and planting a vineyard highlights her financial acumen and long-term vision, qualities often erased or downplayed in patriarchal readings of the text.

Her entrepreneurial spirit extends further, as the text notes her role in commerce: "She sees that her trading is profitable, and her lamp does not go out at night" (Proverbs 31:18). She is depicted as someone who not only participates in the marketplace but excels in it, managing her time and resources with diligence and skill. Far from being confined to domestic labor, the Proverbs 31 woman engages in economic activities that allow her to thrive independently, contributing significantly to the prosperity of her household. This entrepreneurial success, described as profitable and illuminating, underscores her capacity as a leader and innovator.

The independence of the Proverbs 31 woman is also evident in the way she commands respect and wields influence. "She is clothed with strength and dignity; she can laugh at the days to come" (Proverbs 31:25). This is a woman who moves through the world with confidence and assurance, unburdened by fear or uncertainty. Her strength and dignity are not derived from submission but from her ability to navigate challenges, make decisions, and secure her family's well-being. Her laughter in the face of the future reflects her self-reliance and preparedness—a stark contrast to the narrative of dependence often ascribed to her.

Additionally, the Proverbs 31 woman is not limited to her household but is deeply engaged in her community. "She opens her arms to the poor and extends her hands to the needy" (Proverbs 31:20). This highlights her role as a benefactor and leader, someone who uses her resources and influence to uplift others. Her actions demonstrate that her impact is not confined to her family but reaches outward, embodying a holistic vision of leadership and care that transcends traditional gender roles.

Liberating Proverbs 31 from patriarchal interpretations means reclaiming these qualities, entrepreneurial skill, independence, and community engagement, as central to the text. The woman described here is not a static figure, defined by service and submission, but a dynamic force whose contributions reshape and expand the possibilities for what women can achieve. By emphasizing her entrepreneurial and independent aspects, we challenge the reductive narratives that have used Proverbs 31 to confine women and instead celebrate it as a testament to their power and potential. This reinterpretation transforms the text into a source of empowerment, offering a liberatory vision that affirms women's agency, leadership, and capacity for transformation.

Modern Applications

A liberated reading of Proverbs 31 reclaims the text from its patriarchal distortions, offering contemporary women a powerful framework for empowerment, agency, and leadership. By emphasizing the entrepreneurial, independent, and community-focused aspects of the Proverbs 31 woman, this interpretation shifts the narrative from one of restriction to one of liberation. In doing so, it inspires women to embrace their multifaceted identities, pursue their ambitions unapologetically, and challenge the societal norms that seek to confine them.

At its core, a liberated reading of Proverbs 31 reframes the woman described in the text as a model of strength, resourcefulness, and influence. This reimagining resonates with modern women who navigate complex and intersecting roles in their lives, as professionals, caregivers, activists, and leaders. By recognizing that the Proverbs 31 woman is more than a domestic caretaker, contemporary women can see their own contributions in a new light. Whether managing a household, running a business, or advocating for social change, women can find affirmation in her example, knowing that their efforts are valuable and transformative.

One of the most significant ways this reinterpretation empowers contemporary women is by challenging the idea that their worth is tied solely to traditional roles. Patriarchal readings of Proverbs 31 have long emphasized domesticity and submission, creating unrealistic and oppressive standards for women. A liberated reading rejects these narrow expectations, highlighting the Proverbs 31 woman's autonomy and versatility. This shift encourages modern women to pursue paths that align with their unique skills and passions, whether those paths lead to entrepreneurship, academia, activism, or other endeavors. It reinforces the idea that women are not defined by any single role but by the fullness of their contributions and aspirations.

Furthermore, this reading offers a counter-narrative to the culture of perfectionism that has been perpetuated by traditional interpretations of Proverbs 31. Many women feel the pressure to "do it all" and "be it all," striving to meet unattainable ideals of perfection. A liberated understanding of the text emphasizes not perfection but purpose and authenticity. The Proverbs 31 woman is not a one-dimensional figure; she is a dynamic individual whose actions reflect her values and priorities. This perspective empowers contemporary women to define success on their own terms, rejecting the societal pressures that demand conformity and self-sacrifice at the expense of personal growth and fulfillment.

A liberated reading of Proverbs 31 also inspires women to engage with their communities and the world around them. The text describes a woman who uses her resources to uplift others, extending her hands to the poor and speaking wisdom in public spaces. This example challenges modern women to see their leadership as not only a personal endeavor but also a means of creating positive change in their communities. By reclaiming this vision of leadership, women can feel empowered to advocate for justice, build networks of support, and mentor others, fostering a sense of collective empowerment.

Finally, this reinterpretation encourages women to embrace their spirituality as a source of strength and resilience. The Proverbs 31 woman's faith is central to her identity, grounding her actions and inspiring her confidence. A liberated reading affirms that spirituality is not a tool for enforcing submission but a foundation for empowerment and transformation. It invites women to explore their faith in ways that affirm their dignity, challenge oppression, and inspire action.

In a world that continues to place barriers in the way of women's equality, a liberated reading of Proverbs 31 is a radical act of reclamation. It empowers contemporary women to see themselves as agents of change, worthy of respect and capable of greatness in every sphere of life. By rejecting the limitations imposed by patriarchal interpretations, women can embrace the Proverbs 31 woman as a model of courage, wisdom, and impact, a figure whose legacy challenges us all to live boldly, lead fearlessly, and love fully.

Paul's Letters - Lost in Patriarchal Translation
Paul's Influence

The Apostle Paul stands as one of the most influential figures in early
Christianity, a prolific writer whose letters shaped the theology, ethics,
and practices of the emerging church. His writings, found throughout
the New Testament, reflect a complex and dynamic engagement with
the cultural, social, and spiritual issues of his time. Paul's letters
provided guidance to early Christian communities, navigating their
struggles to live faithfully amidst Roman imperialism, cultural
diversity, and internal discord. However, over centuries, Paul's words
have been selectively interpreted and weaponized by patriarchal
systems to entrench gender hierarchies, silence women, and restrict
their roles within both the church and society.

Paul's influence cannot be overstated. His letters, including those to
the Corinthians, Ephesians, and Romans, form a substantial portion
of the New Testament and have been a cornerstone of Christian
teaching for millennia. These writings, deeply rooted in the context of
their time, addressed the specific needs and challenges of early
Christian communities. Paul's themes of grace, faith, and unity were
revolutionary, offering a vision of a community grounded in Christ
that transcended ethnic, social, and gender divisions. Yet, alongside
these liberatory ideas, his writings also contain passages that, when
read through a patriarchal lens, have been used to justify the
exclusion and subordination of women.

Perhaps the most cited of Paul's controversial statements appears in 1
Corinthians 14:34-35, where he writes, "Women should remain silent
in the churches. They are not allowed to speak but must be in
submission, as the law says." This passage has been interpreted as a
blanket prohibition on women speaking or leading within church
settings, forming the basis for centuries of exclusion from ecclesiastical
authority. Similarly, in 1 Timothy 2:11-12, attributed to Paul though
likely written by a later disciple, the author states, "I do not permit a
woman to teach or to assume authority over a man; she must be
quiet." These verses have been used to build entire doctrines that
confine women to roles of obedience and silence, framing such
restrictions as divinely ordained.

What is often overlooked in these interpretations is the cultural and historical context of Paul's letters. Paul was writing to communities navigating the complexities of a patriarchal Greco-Roman world, where social norms were deeply entrenched in hierarchical structures. His instructions often reflect a pragmatic approach to fostering unity and stability within these communities, addressing specific situations rather than establishing universal doctrines. For instance, the silence prescribed in 1 Corinthians 14 is part of a broader discussion on orderly worship, and its application may have been intended to address particular disruptions rather than impose a lasting rule.

Moreover, patriarchal readings of Paul ignore the many instances in which he affirms women's leadership and contributions to the church. In Romans 16, Paul commends several women, including Phoebe, a deacon, and Junia, described as "outstanding among the apostles." These examples suggest that Paul recognized and valued the leadership roles women played in the early Christian movement, challenging the notion that his writings endorse their exclusion.

The co-opting of Paul's letters by patriarchal systems reflects a broader tendency to selectively emphasize certain passages while ignoring others that undermine hierarchical interpretations. By framing Paul as a proponent of male dominance, patriarchal theology has perpetuated a distorted understanding of his teachings, using his words to justify inequality rather than unity. This selective reading not only misrepresents Paul's vision but also undermines the transformative potential of his message, a message rooted in the radical inclusivity of the gospel.

To engage with Paul's letters critically is to recognize their complexity and context, rejecting simplistic interpretations that serve oppressive agendas. Paul's writings, when read with a focus on their historical and cultural backdrop, reveal a nuanced and often liberatory perspective that challenges rather than reinforces patriarchal norms. Recovering this perspective is essential to reclaiming Paul's legacy as a figure who, despite his contradictions, envisioned a community where all are equal in Christ.

## Silencing Women

The directive in 1 Corinthians 14:34–35, where Paul writes, "Women should remain silent in the churches. They are not allowed to speak but must be in submission, as the law says," has been one of the most controversial and frequently cited passages used to restrict women's roles within the church. Over centuries, this verse has become a cornerstone of doctrines that silence women, barring them from preaching, leadership, and even participation in theological discourse. However, a closer examination of its cultural and historical context reveals that this interpretation is far from straightforward and that the passage itself may reflect specific, localized concerns rather than a universal principle.

To begin with, it is essential to situate this passage within the broader context of 1 Corinthians. Paul's letter addresses a diverse and fractious Christian community in Corinth, one grappling with issues of unity, worship, and social dynamics. The directive for women to remain silent appears in a section about orderly worship, suggesting that it is part of a broader conversation about maintaining structure and avoiding disruptions during gatherings. It is not an isolated command but one embedded within a series of instructions aimed at fostering harmony in a context where disorder could undermine the community's witness and cohesion.

The cultural context of the Greco-Roman world further illuminates this passage. Corinth was a bustling, cosmopolitan city where public life was dominated by patriarchal norms, and women's visibility in public spaces was often viewed with suspicion or hostility. In such a setting, women speaking publicly in a religious assembly could be perceived as disruptive or even scandalous, threatening the community's social standing and credibility. Paul's directive may have been a pragmatic response to these cultural realities, aimed at protecting the fledgling Christian movement from external criticism or internal division. This reading suggests that the silence was not intended as a permanent theological mandate but as a contextual guideline addressing a specific situation.

Additionally, the phrase "as the law says" raises questions about its origin and application. There is no direct reference in Jewish or Roman law that explicitly commands women to remain silent. This ambiguity has led some scholars to propose that Paul was quoting or responding to a local tradition or belief, rather than asserting a divine command. Others suggest that this phrase reflects an interpolation, a later addition by scribes seeking to align Paul's writings with emerging patriarchal norms in the early church. While this remains speculative, it underscores the complexities of interpreting this passage and the need for caution in applying it universally.

It is also significant to consider the tension between this directive and other parts of Paul's letters where he acknowledges and even celebrates women's active roles in the church. In 1 Corinthians 11:5, Paul refers to women praying and prophesying in worship, implying their vocal participation. In Romans 16, he commends women like Phoebe, a deacon, and Junia, whom he calls "outstanding among the apostles." These examples suggest that Paul did not uniformly silence women but recognized and valued their contributions to the early Christian movement. The apparent contradiction highlights the importance of context and the possibility that 1 Corinthians 14:34–35 reflects a situational response rather than a universal principle.

Finally, the directive to silence women must be understood in light of the gospel's broader themes of liberation and equality. Paul himself writes in Galatians 3:28, "There is neither Jew nor Gentile, neither slave nor free, nor is there male and female, for you are all one in Christ Jesus." This vision of unity and equality stands in stark contrast to interpretations that use 1 Corinthians 14 to enforce gendered hierarchies. Reconciling these tensions requires a critical and contextual reading that resists reductive or oppressive applications.

Dissecting the cultural and historical contexts of 1 Corinthians 14:34–35 reveals the limitations of using this passage to silence women universally. Rather than a timeless command, it reflects a specific and pragmatic response to the challenges faced by the Corinthian church. Recovering this nuance allows for a reading of scripture that affirms women's voices and leadership, aligning with the liberatory message of the gospel rather than the constraints of patriarchal tradition.

Reinterpreting Paul

Paul's writings, often wielded to exclude women from leadership and participation in the church, reveal a more complex and inclusive perspective when read critically and contextually. Far from being a blanket endorsement of patriarchy, Paul's letters offer numerous examples of women serving as leaders, teachers, and apostles within early Christian communities. Reinterpreting Paul's intent through a progressive lens highlights his recognition of women's vital contributions to the faith, challenging the restrictive readings that have historically silenced their voices.

One of the clearest examples of Paul's recognition of women as leaders is found in Romans 16, where he commends several women by name for their roles in the church. Phoebe, described as a "deacon" and a benefactor of many, is entrusted by Paul to deliver his letter to the Roman church. The term "deacon" (diakonos) signifies a position of responsibility and service, indicating that Phoebe was not merely a helper but a leader within her community. Paul's trust in her to carry and possibly explain his theological message to the Roman congregation underscores her authority and capability.

Another striking example is Junia, mentioned in Romans 16:7 as "outstanding among the apostles." For centuries, Junia's identity as a woman was obscured by patriarchal interpretations that altered her name to the masculine "Junias," an effort to erase the possibility of a female apostle. However, scholarship has since confirmed Junia's gender, restoring her rightful place as a prominent leader in the early church. Paul's acknowledgment of Junia as an apostle, a title denoting significant authority and witness to the risen Christ, challenges the notion that he opposed women in positions of leadership.

Beyond individual examples, Paul's broader theological vision affirms the equality of all believers. In Galatians 3:28, he declares, "There is neither Jew nor Gentile, neither slave nor free, nor is there male and female, for you are all one in Christ Jesus." This statement encapsulates the radical inclusivity of the gospel, rejecting divisions based on ethnicity, social status, or gender. While Paul's practical instructions often reflect the patriarchal norms of his time, his theological framework points toward a community where such hierarchies are ultimately dismantled.

The tension between Paul's affirmations of women's leadership and his more restrictive statements, such as those in 1 Corinthians 14 or 1 Timothy 2, reflects the challenges of interpreting his letters. These passages, often cited to silence women, must be understood in their specific historical and cultural contexts. For instance, Paul's instruction for women to remain silent in church may have been a pragmatic response to particular disruptions in worship rather than a universal command. Similarly, the directive for women to learn "in quietness and full submission" (1 Timothy 2:11) reflects the societal norms of the Greco-Roman world, where women's public roles were limited. These instructions were likely context-specific and should not overshadow the broader themes of equality and inclusion in Paul's writings.

Reinterpreting Paul's intent involves reclaiming the liberatory elements of his letters while critically examining the cultural biases that have shaped their interpretation. Paul's recognition of women as leaders, teachers, and apostles in the early church provides a foundation for affirming their roles in contemporary faith communities. His theological vision of unity and equality calls us to challenge patriarchal structures that contradict the gospel's inclusive message. By embracing a progressive understanding of Paul's writings, we honor the diverse contributions of women in the early church and reaffirm their rightful place as leaders in the ongoing work of faith and justice.

Broader Challenges

Reclaiming biblical texts like Paul's letters from the grip of patriarchal institutions is a daunting but essential task. These texts have been entrenched in theological frameworks and cultural norms that, for centuries, have used scripture to justify the subjugation of women and the reinforcement of rigid gender hierarchies. The challenge lies not only in confronting deeply ingrained interpretations but also in dismantling the structures of power that perpetuate these distortions. Yet, the difficulty of this work underscores its importance, as reclaiming these texts is a critical step toward liberating them from their misuse and restoring their transformative potential.

One of the primary challenges in reclaiming patriarchally entrenched texts is their long history of selective interpretation. Passages such as 1 Corinthians 14:34–35 ("women should remain silent in the churches") or 1 Timothy 2:11–12 ("I do not permit a woman to teach or to assume authority over a man") have been lifted from their historical and cultural contexts and weaponized to silence women. These verses are often emphasized at the expense of others that affirm women's roles as leaders and equal participants in the faith, such as Paul's acknowledgment of Phoebe as a deacon and Junia as an apostle in Romans 16. The disproportionate focus on restrictive passages has created a theological bias that is deeply entrenched in church doctrine and tradition.

Compounding this issue is the authority wielded by institutions that uphold patriarchal interpretations of scripture. Religious hierarchies, particularly in denominations that exclude women from leadership roles, have vested interests in maintaining these interpretations, as they reinforce their own structures of power. Attempts to challenge or reinterpret such passages are often met with resistance, labeled as heretical or dismissed as the influence of secular feminism. This institutional gatekeeping stifles critical engagement with scripture, perpetuating a cycle in which patriarchal readings are normalized and dissenting voices marginalized.

The pervasive influence of patriarchal interpretations also presents a cultural challenge. These readings have seeped into societal norms and expectations, shaping attitudes toward gender roles both within and beyond religious communities. Women are often taught to internalize these messages, viewing submission and silence as virtues and questioning their own worth or capabilities. This internalized oppression makes it difficult to envision alternative interpretations, as the patriarchal framework feels not only authoritative but inevitable. Reclaiming texts requires dismantling not only institutional barriers but also the cultural narratives that reinforce them.

Another obstacle is the complexity of scripture itself. Paul's letters, for instance, reflect a mix of liberatory and restrictive themes, written to address specific issues within early Christian communities. Extracting their original intent requires careful analysis of historical, social, and linguistic contexts, as well as an awareness of how these contexts differ from contemporary realities. Patriarchal institutions often exploit the ambiguities and contradictions within these texts to bolster their interpretations, making it difficult to present a cohesive counter-narrative.

Despite these challenges, reclaiming patriarchally entrenched texts is both possible and necessary. Feminist theologians, biblical scholars, and faith leaders have made significant strides in offering alternative readings that emphasize the liberatory and egalitarian aspects of scripture. These interpretations invite believers to see texts not as static commands but as dynamic, contextual writings capable of inspiring justice and equality. This work is an act of resistance, reclaiming scripture from those who have used it as a tool of oppression and restoring its potential to transform lives and communities.

The process of reclaiming these texts is not about erasing their complexity or ignoring their difficult passages but about confronting them honestly and reinterpreting them through a lens of liberation. It requires courage, persistence, and a commitment to truth. While the challenge is immense, so too is the reward: a faith tradition that upholds the dignity, worth, and agency of all people, free from the constraints of patriarchal distortion. This vision is worth the struggle, for it aligns with the deepest callings of scripture itself, justice, equality, and love.

Mary and Mary Magdalene - Subversive Icons
The Marian Dichotomy

The figures of the Virgin Mary and Mary Magdalene stand at the center of Christian tradition, yet their portrayals have been shaped and distorted to serve patriarchal agendas. These two Marys, pivotal in the Gospel narratives, have been framed as contrasting archetypes of idealized womanhood, each embodying a role that reinforces patriarchal control. The Virgin Mary is cast as the epitome of submissive purity, the obedient servant of God, while Mary Magdalene is characterized as the repentant sinner, redeemed by her proximity to Christ. Together, they form a dichotomy that restricts women to a narrow spectrum of roles, submissive or fallen, chaste or redeemed, leaving little room for complexity, agency, or leadership.

The Virgin Mary has long been exalted as the model of feminine virtue, celebrated for her purity, humility, and obedience. In the Annunciation narrative (Luke 1:26–38), Mary's acceptance of her role as the mother of Jesus is often interpreted as an act of total submission: "I am the Lord's servant," she declares. "May your word to me be fulfilled." This statement has been used to portray Mary as the ideal woman, meek, compliant, and entirely devoted to God's will. While her faith and courage are undeniable, patriarchal interpretations of her story have stripped it of its depth, reducing her to a passive vessel through which divine plans are enacted. This framing ignores the radical nature of Mary's choice, her strength in facing societal judgment as an unwed mother, and her active role in the life and ministry of her son. Instead, the emphasis on her purity and obedience has been used to set an unattainable standard for women, conflating holiness with passivity and reinforcing the expectation that women's worth lies in their ability to submit.

In contrast, Mary Magdalene has been cast as the archetypal repentant sinner. Though the Gospels never explicitly identify her as a prostitute, centuries of tradition have conflated her with unnamed sinful women in scripture, a mischaracterization that has persisted in art, literature, and theology. Pope Gregory I's infamous sermon in the 6th century cemented this association, framing Mary Magdalene as a fallen woman redeemed by her repentance and devotion to Christ. This portrayal serves a dual purpose: it reinforces the idea that women's sexuality is inherently sinful and in need of redemption, and it limits women's roles to those of penitent followers rather than active leaders.

This reduction of Mary Magdalene's identity is particularly egregious given her prominent role in the Gospels. She is described as a close companion of Jesus, a witness to his crucifixion, and the first to encounter the risen Christ, earning her the title "apostle to the apostles." These moments highlight her leadership, faith, and significance within the early Christian movement. Yet patriarchal interpretations have downplayed these aspects of her story, focusing instead on her supposed sinfulness and redemption. This framing not only diminishes Mary Magdalene's contributions but also perpetuates the idea that women's spiritual authority is contingent on their repentance and subordination.

The dichotomy between the Virgin Mary and Mary Magdalene creates a restrictive framework for women's identities within Christian tradition. Women are presented with a binary choice: embody the unattainable purity and submission of the Virgin Mary or seek redemption for their inherent sinfulness like Mary Magdalene. This framework erases the complexity and diversity of women's experiences, reducing them to symbols of virtue or vice rather than recognizing their full humanity and agency.

Reclaiming these figures from patriarchal distortion requires reexamining their stories with a focus on their strength, agency, and leadership. The Virgin Mary is not merely a passive vessel but a courageous, active participant in God's plan, who challenges societal norms and speaks prophetically in her Magnificat. Mary Magdalene, far from a repentant outcast, is a leader and witness whose role in the resurrection narrative underscores her authority within the early church. By reclaiming these women as multidimensional figures, we challenge the dichotomy that has confined women for centuries and affirm their rightful place as leaders, visionaries, and full participants in the story of faith.

Mary's Role

The Virgin Mary's story, often overshadowed by patriarchal interpretations that reduce her to a passive vessel of submission, is in fact one of profound resistance and radical agency. Her "yes" to God's plan, spoken during the Annunciation (Luke 1:26–38), is not a mere act of compliance but a bold decision that defies societal norms, embraces immense personal risk, and asserts her role as an active participant in the divine narrative. Far from being a symbol of meekness, Mary emerges as a figure of courage, faith, and revolutionary hope, a woman who reclaims agency in a world that sought to deny it to her.

The Annunciation is often framed as an act of submission, with Mary portrayed as the ideal of feminine obedience. Yet this interpretation overlooks the gravity of her decision and the radical implications of her consent. When the angel Gabriel announces that she will bear the Son of God, Mary is not given a command; she is invited into a partnership. Her response, "I am the Lord's servant. May your word to me be fulfilled," is not the passive acquiescence of someone without choice but the deliberate acceptance of a mission fraught with danger and uncertainty. In a society that stigmatized unwed mothers and could punish them with death, Mary's agreement to carry and raise Jesus was an act of defiance against the cultural expectations and risks of her time.

Mary's decision also reflects a deep trust in God and a willingness to disrupt the status quo. Her Magnificat (Luke 1:46–55), a hymn of praise and prophecy, reveals the revolutionary nature of her faith. In it, she proclaims the downfall of the powerful and the exaltation of the humble, the scattering of the proud and the lifting of the oppressed. These are not the words of a passive figure but of a prophet who understands the transformative power of God's work and her role within it. Mary's song echoes the radical promises of justice and liberation found throughout scripture, positioning her as a central figure in the unfolding story of salvation.

As a young, marginalized woman in a patriarchal society, Mary's "yes" is an assertion of agency in a context that offered her little. She chooses to step into a narrative that will redefine her life and reshape the world. Her role as the mother of Jesus places her at the heart of

God's plan, not as a passive bystander but as an active participant who nurtures, guides, and ultimately witnesses the fulfillment of the promise made to her. Mary's faith is not blind submission but a courageous trust that defies fear and embraces the unknown.

Reclaiming Mary as a symbol of resistance challenges the patriarchal framing that limits her story to one of submission and purity. Her "yes" is not a call for women to accept oppressive circumstances but an invitation to engage fully with the divine work of justice, love, and transformation. Her life demonstrates that faith is not passive but active, requiring boldness, risk, and a commitment to a vision of a better world.

For contemporary women, Mary's radical "yes" serves as a source of empowerment and inspiration. It reminds us that resistance often begins in unexpected places, with individuals who choose courage over comfort, agency over acquiescence. By embracing Mary as a figure of resistance, we reclaim her as a model of strength, vision, and transformative faith, reminding us all of the power of saying "yes" to the work of liberation and justice.

Mary's role as a symbol of resistance also resonates in her steadfastness throughout Jesus' life and ministry. From the nativity to the crucifixion, Mary remains a constant presence, embodying a quiet but unyielding strength in the face of adversity. She challenges the expectations placed upon her, standing at the foot of the cross when others fled and witnessing the culmination of the mission she had courageously embraced. Her unwavering faith and resilience in the most harrowing moments reflect a deep conviction in the transformative power of God's justice and love. Mary's story, therefore, is not just about her initial "yes" but about the enduring commitment to act with courage and compassion in the face of profound personal and social challenges. This makes her not only a figure of historical significance but also a timeless example of the power of resistance rooted in faith and love.

Mary Magdalene's Leadership

Mary Magdalene stands as one of the most significant figures in the Gospel narratives, yet her role as a leader in the early church and witness to the resurrection has often been diminished or overshadowed by patriarchal interpretations. Centuries of distortion, including her wrongful conflation with unnamed sinful women in the Gospels, have reduced her identity to that of a repentant sinner, obscuring her true significance as a faithful disciple and the "apostle to the apostles." By reclaiming her story, we uncover a powerful narrative of leadership, faith, and unwavering devotion that challenges the constraints of patriarchal theology.

The Gospels consistently depict Mary Magdalene as a devoted follower of Jesus, present at critical moments in his ministry, death, and resurrection. She is one of the few named women who travel with Jesus, supporting his mission both spiritually and materially (Luke 8:1–3). Her presence at the crucifixion, when many of the male disciples fled, underscores her courage and loyalty (John 19:25). This steadfastness is further highlighted in her role as the first witness to the resurrection, a moment that places her at the very heart of the Christian faith.

In John 20:1–18, Mary Magdalene is the first to encounter the risen Christ. After discovering the empty tomb, she remains in the garden, weeping, when Jesus appears to her and calls her by name. This intimate moment affirms her unique relationship with Christ and her critical role in the resurrection narrative. Jesus entrusts her with the task of announcing the resurrection to the disciples, saying, "Go to my brothers and tell them" (John 20:17). In this act, Mary becomes the first to proclaim the foundational truth of Christianity, that Jesus has risen. Her title as "apostle to the apostles," bestowed by early Christian theologians, reflects this leadership role, yet patriarchal narratives have often obscured or diminished its significance.

The erasure of Mary Magdalene's leadership is not accidental. It reflects a broader pattern within patriarchal institutions to downplay women's contributions to the early church and to frame them within narrowly defined roles of submission and repentance. The conflation of Mary Magdalene with the unnamed sinful woman in Luke 7:36–50, popularized by Pope Gregory I in the 6th century, is a prime example of this distortion. By casting her as a repentant prostitute rather than a faithful disciple and leader, the church effectively undermined her authority and reframed her story to align with patriarchal ideals of women's virtue as dependent on redemption through male approval.

This mischaracterization not only diminishes Mary Magdalene's leadership but also perpetuates harmful stereotypes about women's moral and spiritual capacities. Her role as the first witness to the resurrection—a position of unparalleled theological significance—is often overshadowed by narratives that emphasize her alleged sinfulness. This selective retelling of her story reinforces the patriarchal framework that limits women's roles within the church and reduces their spiritual contributions to acts of penitence.

Reclaiming Mary Magdalene's leadership is essential to challenging these distortions and restoring her rightful place in the Christian narrative. As the first proclaimer of the resurrection, she exemplifies the courage, faith, and authority that have defined leadership in the church. Her story is a powerful testament to the inclusion and empowerment of women in the early Christian movement, a vision that stands in stark contrast to the exclusionary practices that have dominated much of church history.

Mary Magdalene's leadership also carries profound implications for contemporary faith communities. By recognizing her as a central figure in the resurrection narrative and a leader in the early church, we challenge the patriarchal norms that continue to marginalize women in spiritual spaces. Her story inspires women to claim their voices and leadership, affirming their rightful place as full participants in the ongoing work of faith, justice, and love. Reclaiming Mary Magdalene is not merely an act of historical correction; it is a radical affirmation of the transformative power of women's leadership in the church and the world.

Reclaiming Their Power

Reclaiming the power of the Virgin Mary and Mary Magdalene from centuries of patriarchal distortion reveals their revolutionary potential as figures of courage, leadership, and transformation. When their stories are liberated from the reductive frameworks that have confined them, Mary as the submissive mother and Magdalene as the repentant sinner, they emerge as profound symbols of agency and resistance. These two Marys, central to the Christian narrative, embody the power of faith to challenge oppressive systems and inspire new visions of justice, equality, and liberation.

The Virgin Mary, often depicted as the passive vessel of divine will, is in fact a radical figure of agency and resistance. Her "yes" to God's plan during the Annunciation is not an act of meek submission but a bold decision to embrace a dangerous and uncertain path. As an unwed mother in a patriarchal society, Mary's choice placed her in direct opposition to the cultural norms that sought to control women's bodies and lives. Her Magnificat, a hymn of revolutionary hope, proclaims the overthrow of the powerful and the upliftment of the marginalized, aligning her story with the broader scriptural themes of liberation and justice. When freed from patriarchal interpretations, Mary is no longer a symbol of compliance but a model of transformative faith and courage, inspiring women to claim their agency and defy societal constraints.

Mary Magdalene, likewise, transcends the distortions that have cast her as a repentant sinner dependent on Christ's forgiveness. In reality, she is a leader, a witness, and an apostle to the apostles. Her role as the first to encounter the risen Christ and proclaim the resurrection places her at the heart of the Christian message, a position of unparalleled theological significance. Reclaiming Magdalene's story as one of leadership and faith challenges the patriarchal narratives that have sought to erase women's contributions to the early church. Her example empowers women to see themselves not as secondary or subordinate but as active participants in the work of spiritual transformation and social justice.

The revolutionary potential of these figures lies not only in their individual stories but also in the broader implications of reclaiming them. By restoring the Virgin Mary and Mary Magdalene to their rightful places as agents of change, we disrupt the frameworks that have long restricted women's roles in religious and societal contexts. Their stories remind us that faith is not about passivity or submission but about courage, action, and the willingness to challenge unjust systems. They call us to reject the binaries that confine women, pure or fallen, submissive or rebellious, and to embrace the fullness of their humanity and potential.

Reclaiming these figures also serves as a broader critique of the patriarchal structures that have shaped religious interpretation. It challenges the authority of institutions that have used scripture to silence women and perpetuate inequality, calling instead for a faith that affirms dignity, inclusion, and justice. The Virgin Mary and Mary Magdalene, when freed from patriarchal distortions, become symbols of a faith tradition that values women's voices, leadership, and contributions, a tradition that reflects the liberatory spirit of the Gospel itself.

For contemporary women, these reclaimed stories offer both inspiration and empowerment. Mary's courage to say "yes" to the unknown and Magdalene's steadfast proclamation of the resurrection remind us that resistance and leadership are acts of faith. They invite us to imagine a world where women's power is not constrained by societal norms but celebrated as a force for transformation. By reclaiming their power, we honor their legacy and affirm the revolutionary potential of faith to create a more just and equitable world.

Conclusion - Toward a Liberatory Theology
Connecting the Threads

The journey through these chapters reveals a single, resounding truth: the Bible, when stripped of patriarchal distortions and reclaimed with courage and critical insight, holds immense liberatory potential. From Genesis to the letters of Paul, from the Proverbs 31 woman to the stories of Mary and Mary Magdalene, scripture emerges not as a tool of subjugation but as a vibrant, living testament to the transformative power of faith, agency, and justice. The task of deconstructing entrenched interpretations and reclaiming these texts is not merely an academic exercise, it is an act of resistance, a refusal to allow the sacred to be monopolized by systems of oppression. It is a call to rediscover the radical promise of scripture as a source of empowerment and liberation.

At the heart of this endeavor is the recognition that patriarchal interpretations of the Bible are not inherent to the text itself but are products of historical and cultural contexts shaped by power and control. These distortions have silenced women, erased their contributions, and framed their worth through narrow, confining lenses. Yet, as we have seen, the stories of Eve, the Proverbs 31 woman, the Virgin Mary, and Mary Magdalene offer a counter-narrative, one that celebrates agency, leadership, and the courage to challenge oppressive norms. These figures, reclaimed from centuries of patriarchal misuse, stand as powerful symbols of what faith can inspire: the boldness to question, the strength to endure, and the vision to create change.

The liberatory potential of scripture lies in its contradictions and complexities, which invite interpretation, engagement, and transformation. The stories of Genesis challenge us to reframe Eve not as a sinner but as a seeker of knowledge and agency. Proverbs 31, when freed from the constraints of patriarchal expectations, becomes a celebration of women's independence and resourcefulness. Paul's letters, often used to silence women, reveal a vision of unity and equality that undermines the very hierarchies they have been used to enforce. And the lives of Mary and Mary Magdalene, stripped of distortions, offer profound examples of faith and leadership that defy the limits placed upon them by history.

Together, these reclaimed narratives weave a tapestry of resistance and hope. They affirm that faith is not about passivity or submission but about engagement, transformation, and justice. They remind us that scripture does not belong to the powerful or the gatekeepers of tradition, it belongs to the people, to those who dare to wrestle with its meaning and reclaim its promises for the marginalized and oppressed. This reclamation is not about rewriting scripture but about rediscovering its depth and allowing it to speak anew to the challenges of our time.

The work of building a liberatory theology does not end with reclaiming these texts, it begins there. A deconstructed and reclaimed biblical tradition calls us to action, to embody the values of justice, love, and equality that pulse through its stories. It challenges us to confront the systems of oppression that persist in our world, from gender inequality to racial injustice, and to imagine communities that reflect the radical inclusivity of the Gospel. It invites us to see faith not as a static set of beliefs but as a dynamic, evolving force for transformation.

In reclaiming scripture, we reclaim our right to tell our own stories, to challenge the narratives that confine us, and to envision a future where justice and liberation are not just ideals but realities. This is the promise of a liberatory theology: a faith that uplifts rather than oppresses, that empowers rather than silences, and that seeks to heal and transform the world. It is a call to each of us to participate in this work, to bring our voices, our questions, and our hopes to the sacred texts that have shaped us, and to find in them the seeds of a more just and compassionate future.

Call to Action

The work of reclaiming sacred texts from the grip of patriarchal interpretations is not limited to scholars or theologians; it is a collective effort, and it begins with you. The stories and themes explored in this book are not simply relics of the past but living tools for challenging oppression and building a more just and equitable world. The call to action is clear: engage critically with scripture, confront the distortions that have been used to silence and subjugate, and reclaim the liberatory potential of these texts in your own life and community.

The Bible has too often been wielded as a weapon to uphold systems of power and control, its messages of justice, love, and equality buried beneath centuries of selective interpretation. But it does not have to remain this way. As readers, we have the power and responsibility to wrestle with these texts, to ask hard questions, and to challenge interpretations that harm rather than heal. This work requires courage, for it means confronting not only institutional authority but also the internalized narratives that have shaped our understanding of faith and identity. Yet this courage is what transforms scripture from a tool of oppression into a source of liberation.

Begin by reading scripture with fresh eyes, approaching it not as a static set of commands but as a dynamic, complex collection of stories, poems, and teachings. Pay attention to the voices that have been silenced, the women, the marginalized, the outcasts, and consider how their stories challenge the hierarchies that have sought to erase them. Engage with the text critically, examining its historical and cultural contexts while also allowing it to speak to the realities of today. Ask yourself: Whose interests does this interpretation serve? Whose voices are missing? How can this story be reclaimed to inspire justice and equality?

Next, bring these questions into your community. Whether in a church, a study group, or a circle of friends, create spaces where scripture can be discussed openly and critically. Share the stories of figures like Eve, Mary Magdalene, and the Proverbs 31 woman as they truly are, complex, dynamic, and revolutionary. Challenge teachings that reduce these figures to stereotypes or use their narratives to reinforce oppressive norms. Encourage dialogue that affirms the dignity and leadership of women and other marginalized groups, creating a culture of inclusion and empowerment.

This call to action extends beyond interpretation to advocacy. Scripture has been used to justify countless injustices, from gender inequality to racial oppression to economic exploitation. Reclaiming its liberatory potential means using its messages of justice and love to challenge these systems in the world around us. Speak out against policies and practices that perpetuate harm, and use the language of faith to advocate for equity and compassion. Just as the Gospel calls us to care for the least of these, it also calls us to dismantle the structures that create "the least" in the first place.

Remember that reclaiming sacred texts is not an act of destruction but of restoration. It is about peeling back the layers of distortion to uncover the radical messages of hope and transformation that lie within. It is about affirming that scripture belongs to all of us, not just to those in power, and that its stories have the power to inspire change when read critically and courageously.

The work of engaging with scripture is ongoing, a journey rather than a destination. It invites each of us to bring our questions, our struggles, and our hopes to the text, trusting that in its complexity we will find both challenge and inspiration. By taking up this call, you join a movement that refuses to allow the sacred to be used as a weapon of harm and instead reclaims it as a tool for healing and justice.

This call to action also demands that we confront the institutions and traditions that have perpetuated patriarchal interpretations of scripture. Religious hierarchies often resist change, clinging to interpretations that reinforce their power. Challenging these structures may feel daunting, but change begins with persistent voices and collective effort. Advocate for greater representation of women and marginalized groups in leadership within your faith community. Question practices and teachings that exclude or diminish others, and push for reform that reflects the radical inclusivity and justice of the Gospel. Remember, institutions only change when those within them demand accountability and transformation.

Equally important is the need to reclaim sacred texts in personal and family spaces. Begin by reintroducing scripture as a source of liberation and inspiration rather than one of fear or control. Teach the next generation to read critically, to see figures like Eve and Mary Magdalene as symbols of agency and leadership rather than cautionary tales of disobedience or sin. Encourage young people to question and engage with scripture, fostering a sense of ownership and curiosity rather than blind obedience. By equipping them with the tools to interpret texts critically, we prepare them to challenge oppressive narratives and build a faith tradition that uplifts rather than diminishes.

Finally, let this call to action be a reminder that reclaiming scripture is a profoundly hopeful endeavor. It is a declaration that the stories of our faith, no matter how misused or distorted, still hold the power to inspire transformation. It is an affirmation that the voices of the silenced and marginalized can be amplified and honored, that the sacred can be a source of healing rather than harm. This hope fuels the work ahead, reminding us that we are not just reading these texts but living them, embodying their promises of justice, love, and liberation in our own lives and communities. The sacred is not static; it grows, evolves, and speaks anew in every generation. By answering this call, we become part of that ongoing story. The time to act is now. The work begins with us.

# Part II
## *Reclaiming Power and Spirit*

Introduction to Reclaiming Power and Spirit
Overview

For too long, scripture has been wielded as a weapon to control,
silence, and oppress, particularly for women whose lives and voices
have been shaped, and often stifled, by patriarchal interpretations.
These interpretations, deeply entrenched in religious traditions, have
presented sacred texts as immutable decrees that reinforce gender
hierarchies and restrict women's roles to the margins of spiritual and
societal life. Yet, this is not the true nature of scripture. Beneath the
layers of distortion lies a transformative power, a power that speaks to
justice, equality, and liberation. Reclaiming scripture as a tool for
empowerment is not only possible but essential, especially for those
who have been told for generations that the divine does not include or
celebrate them in full.

The Bible's stories, teachings, and poetry are alive with complexity,
contradiction, and nuance. They are not static blueprints for
domination but dynamic texts shaped by their historical and cultural
contexts. For women, reclaiming these texts means peeling back the
layers of patriarchal distortion and reinterpreting them through a lens
of resistance and liberation. It means moving beyond the restrictive
frameworks that limit women to roles of submission, repentance, or
service and uncovering the profound messages of strength, agency,
and justice that permeate the scriptures. It is a bold act of faith, an
assertion that the sacred belongs not to the powerful few but to all of
us, and that its stories can inspire the work of transformation and
healing.

This reclamation begins with the recognition that patriarchal
interpretations are neither divine nor inevitable. They are human
constructs, shaped by the historical and social realities of those who
sought to use scripture to consolidate power. These interpretations
have often emphasized passages that reinforce male dominance while
ignoring or minimizing texts that celebrate women's leadership,
wisdom, and courage. The result is a theological tradition that frames
women as inherently secondary, temptresses like Eve, penitents like
Mary Magdalene, or helpers like the Proverbs 31 woman, valued only
in their roles as wives, mothers, or servants. Reclaiming scripture
involves challenging these narrow narratives and reclaiming the
fullness of the biblical witness, which includes stories of women who

defy norms, lead with conviction, and embody the liberatory spirit of
the divine.

Central to this work is the idea of resistance. Patriarchal systems rely
on the passive acceptance of their interpretations to maintain control,
and scripture has often been used to justify this submission. Women
have been told to accept their "place" in the divine order, to remain
silent in worship, to submit to male authority as an act of faith. But
resistance is also an act of faith, a refusal to accept interpretations that
harm and diminish, and a commitment to uncovering the truth that
sets us free. The Bible itself is filled with stories of resistance: the
midwives who defied Pharaoh's command to kill Hebrew infants,
Esther's courage in confronting the king, Mary's radical "yes" to a
plan that defied societal expectations, and Mary Magdalene's
steadfast witness to the resurrection. These stories remind us that faith
is not about compliance but about courage, action, and the pursuit of
justice.

Reclaiming scripture also involves embracing its liberatory potential.
For women, this means finding in its pages the inspiration to
challenge oppression, to build communities of mutual support, and to
imagine new possibilities for their lives and their faith. The Psalms, for
example, offer prayers of lament and protest that give voice to the
pain of injustice and the hope for deliverance. The story of the
Exodus, long a symbol of liberation, invites women to see themselves
as participants in a divine journey toward freedom. The teachings of
Jesus, who consistently uplifted the marginalized and challenged
societal norms, provide a model for dismantling hierarchies and
affirming the dignity of all people.

The work of reclaiming scripture is deeply personal but also
profoundly communal. It is not enough for individual women to find
liberation in these texts; the larger structures of oppression must also
be confronted and transformed. This requires creating spaces where
scripture can be read, discussed, and interpreted collectively, spaces
that welcome questions, honor diverse experiences, and resist the
pressure to conform to traditional narratives. It means fostering
communities that value women's voices and leadership, that affirm
their right to speak, preach, and lead in both spiritual and secular
contexts. By doing so, we reclaim not only the texts but also the spaces

where they are engaged, ensuring that they become tools for empowerment rather than oppression.

This work is not without its challenges. The weight of tradition, the resistance of institutions, and the internalized narratives of inadequacy and guilt can make the process of reclamation difficult. Yet, the very act of engaging with scripture critically and courageously is itself an act of liberation. It is a declaration that the divine is not confined to patriarchal interpretations and that the sacred cannot be monopolized by systems of control. It is a reminder that scripture is alive, dynamic, and capable of inspiring new visions of justice and equality when read with open hearts and minds.

Reclaiming scripture as a tool for empowerment is not merely an intellectual exercise; it is a spiritual and political act of defiance. It affirms that faith is not a weapon of oppression but a source of hope and strength. It invites women to see themselves as full participants in the divine story, not as secondary characters but as leaders, prophets, and visionaries. It challenges us all to reject interpretations that harm and to embrace those that heal, to create communities where the sacred inspires liberation rather than submission.

As we embark on this journey of reclaiming power and spirit, let us remember that the work of faith is not static, it is dynamic, evolving, and deeply connected to the struggles and hopes of the present. Scripture, when freed from patriarchal distortions, has the power to transform lives, communities, and the world. This is the promise of a reclaimed faith: a tradition that uplifts, empowers, and calls us to the work of justice, love, and liberation.

The Psalms of Protest
Historical Context

The Psalms, often called the songbook of the Bible, are among the
most evocative and personal expressions of faith in scripture. These
poetic texts span a vast range of human emotion—from joy and
gratitude to despair and protest. While they are often read as sources
of comfort and inspiration, the Psalms are also deeply rooted in the
historical and social struggles of oppressed communities. They are not
just songs of praise; they are cries of lament, voices raised against
injustice, and expressions of hope in the face of overwhelming odds.
To reclaim the Psalms as tools of resistance and liberation is to
reconnect with their origins as the spiritual lifeblood of a people
navigating the complexities of suffering, resilience, and divine justice.

The historical context of the Psalms is key to understanding their
radical potential. Written over centuries, these texts reflect the
experiences of the ancient Israelites as they faced oppression, exile,
and the constant threat of cultural and political annihilation. The
Psalms were born out of a world where power was concentrated in the
hands of empires that sought to dominate and erase smaller nations.
For the Israelites, who often found themselves at the mercy of these
empires, the Psalms became a means of survival, a way to process
their pain, assert their identity, and cry out to a God they believed
was still present amidst their suffering.

Psalms of lament, in particular, give voice to the anguish of oppressed
communities. Texts like Psalm 13, which begins with the desperate
question, "How long, O Lord? Will you forget me forever?" resonate
with the feelings of abandonment and despair experienced by those
who endure systemic injustice. These Psalms do not shy away from
raw emotion or difficult questions; they confront God directly,
demanding answers and intervention. They are acts of spiritual
defiance, refusing to accept silence or indifference in the face of
suffering. For those who feel unheard in their struggles, these texts
offer validation and a framework for expressing pain without shame.

Yet the Psalms are not merely expressions of despair; they are also
declarations of hope and trust in the possibility of divine justice. Even
in the depths of lament, there is often a turn toward confidence in
God's power to redeem and restore. Psalm 22, for example, begins

with the haunting cry, "My God, my God, why have you forsaken me?" but ends with a vision of deliverance and praise. This movement from lament to hope reflects the resilience of oppressed communities who, despite their circumstances, cling to the belief that justice is possible and that their cries will not go unanswered.

The Psalms also serve as collective expressions of resistance. While many are deeply personal, others, like Psalm 137, reflect communal grief and outrage. Written during the Babylonian exile, Psalm 137 captures the pain of displacement and the yearning for liberation: "By the rivers of Babylon we sat and wept when we remembered Zion." This lament is not only an expression of sorrow but also an act of defiance, refusing to forget their identity or accept their exile as the final word. The communal nature of these Psalms reminds us that lament is not just an individual act but a shared practice that unites communities in their struggles and aspirations.

For contemporary readers, reclaiming the Psalms as texts of protest and hope offers a powerful way to engage with issues of justice and oppression. They remind us that faith does not require the suppression of anger, grief, or doubt; instead, it invites us to bring these emotions into our spiritual practice, to name injustice, and to cry out for change. The Psalms teach us that lament and hope are not opposites but intertwined expressions of a faith that seeks both to confront the realities of suffering and to imagine a better future. Reclaiming their historical context as voices of the oppressed reconnects us with their liberatory potential, transforming them into tools for resistance, resilience, and renewal in our own struggles for justice.

Resistance through Prayer

The Psalms offer profound frameworks for articulating resistance against injustice, embodying the raw honesty and unflinching hope of oppressed communities. Among these, Psalms 13 and 22 stand out as vivid examples of how prayer becomes an act of defiance, a way to confront both human and divine silence in the face of suffering while demanding justice and redemption. These Psalms remind us that resistance is not only a physical or political act but also a spiritual one, rooted in the courage to voice anguish, question injustice, and envision a better future.

Psalm 13 begins with a searing cry: "How long, O Lord? Will you forget me forever? How long will you hide your face from me?" These opening lines capture the despair of feeling abandoned by both God and the world, a sentiment that resonates deeply with those facing systemic oppression or personal suffering. The repetition of "how long" underscores the weight of prolonged injustice, expressing not resignation but the refusal to accept silence as an answer. This Psalm confronts God directly, turning lament into an act of resistance by demanding acknowledgment and action. The psalmist's vulnerability is not a sign of weakness but of profound faith, a belief that even in the depths of despair, God can be called upon to see, hear, and respond.

What makes Psalm 13 particularly powerful as a framework for resistance is its turn from lament to hope. After voicing anguish, the psalmist declares, "But I trust in your unfailing love; my heart rejoices in your salvation." This shift does not erase the pain or injustice expressed earlier but affirms the psalmist's conviction that God's justice will prevail. For those who pray this Psalm, it becomes a way to hold space for both grief and hope, transforming despair into a renewed commitment to faith and action. It teaches that resistance is not only about articulating what is wrong but also about affirming the possibility of change.

Similarly, Psalm 22 begins with a cry of abandonment: "My God, my God, why have you forsaken me?" This opening line, famously echoed by Jesus on the cross, captures the depths of suffering and alienation experienced by those who feel unheard or unseen in their pain. The psalmist vividly describes their anguish, likening themselves

68

to a worm rather than a person, mocked and scorned by those around them. These visceral images reflect the dehumanizing effects of oppression, making this Psalm a powerful voice for those who have been marginalized or silenced.

Yet, like Psalm 13, Psalm 22 does not end in despair. As the Psalm progresses, the tone shifts toward remembrance of God's past faithfulness and a vision of future deliverance. "For he has not despised or scorned the suffering of the afflicted one; he has not hidden his face from him but has listened to his cry for help," declares the psalmist. This affirmation of God's attentiveness transforms the Psalm from a lament into a proclamation of hope and justice. The psalmist envisions a future where all nations acknowledge God's reign, a radical declaration of inclusion and restoration that stands in stark contrast to the isolation described earlier.

Both Psalms 13 and 22 highlight the dual nature of resistance through prayer: they are spaces to name the realities of injustice while simultaneously holding onto the possibility of change. These Psalms do not shy away from hard questions or raw emotions, offering a model for how prayer can be a form of protest. They teach us that faith is not about passive acceptance but about engaging deeply with the complexities of suffering and hope.

For contemporary communities, these Psalms serve as powerful tools for articulating resistance against injustice. They remind us that prayer is not a retreat from the world's struggles but a way to confront them with honesty and courage. By reclaiming these texts, we reclaim the sacred act of crying out against injustice, demanding change, and envisioning a world where justice and love prevail. Through these prayers, resistance becomes a spiritual practice that sustains and empowers us in the ongoing work of liberation.

Reinterpreting the Psalms for Today

The Psalms, written as expressions of lament, praise, and hope, have long served as a spiritual reservoir for those navigating oppression and injustice. Reinterpreted for today, these ancient texts can become prayers for modern resistance, empowering communities to confront systemic injustice with courage, solidarity, and collective action. By adapting their language to contemporary struggles, the Psalms can inspire movements for justice, giving voice to shared grievances and aspirations for a more equitable world. This reimagining transforms the Psalms into tools for collective empowerment, connecting the timeless cries of scripture to the urgent demands of our time.

Consider the themes of solidarity and collective resilience, so central to movements for justice today. A prayer inspired by Psalm 13 might begin with the communal cry, "How long, O God, will injustice reign? How long will the powerful exploit the weak, and the cries of the oppressed go unheard?" This adaptation shifts the Psalm's focus from individual lament to a collective demand for justice, reflecting the interconnected struggles of marginalized communities. It transforms the Psalm into a rallying cry, a call for unity among those who refuse to accept the status quo and believe in the possibility of change.

Modern resistance also requires courage, the willingness to speak truth to power and act boldly in the face of adversity. Psalm 22's opening line, "My God, my God, why have you forsaken me?" captures the isolation and fear that often accompany such struggles. Reimagined for today, it could become a prayer for strength: "My God, in the face of injustice, we feel abandoned. But we will not be silent. Strengthen our voices, embolden our actions, and remind us that we are not alone." This adaptation acknowledges the emotional toll of resistance while affirming the power of perseverance and faith in the face of overwhelming odds.

The Psalms also teach us the importance of collective voices in the pursuit of justice. In movements for change, no single voice can carry the weight of transformation alone; it is the power of many, joined in solidarity, that creates lasting impact. Psalm 137, written from the perspective of a community in exile, can be reinterpreted as a prayer for collective liberation: "By the rivers of despair, we gather and weep, remembering the promises of justice. Together, we lift our voices, refusing to forget who we are and what we fight for. Let our resistance rise like a song of freedom, a melody of hope that cannot be silenced." This modern adaptation honors the communal nature of resistance, highlighting the strength that emerges when individuals unite in pursuit of a shared vision.

Reinterpreted Psalms also affirm the power of hope, even in the face of despair. Psalm 23, with its imagery of God as a shepherd, provides a profound template for resilience: "Even though we walk through the shadow of oppression, we fear no evil, for justice walks beside us, and solidarity strengthens our steps. Surely goodness and freedom will follow us, and together we will dwell in a world made whole." This modern reimagining transforms the Psalm's pastoral imagery into a vision of collective perseverance, reminding us that hope is a vital element of resistance.

By adapting the Psalms into prayers for modern resistance, we breathe new life into these ancient texts, allowing them to speak directly to today's struggles. They become tools for building solidarity, inspiring courage, and amplifying collective voices, connecting the spiritual heritage of scripture to the practical work of justice. In this way, the Psalms continue to fulfill their original purpose: to give voice to those who cry out, to sustain those who resist, and to inspire those who believe in the transformative power of faith and action.

Empowering Women through Psalms

The Psalms, with their raw emotion and unflinching honesty, offer a profound resource for women seeking spiritual strength and empowerment in their personal lives and broader social justice movements. Rooted in the experiences of those who faced oppression and hardship, these ancient prayers provide a framework for connecting with resilience, voicing collective struggles, and mobilizing action. By engaging with the Psalms, women can reclaim their spiritual agency, drawing on these texts to inspire courage, build solidarity, and affirm their role as leaders in the ongoing work of justice and liberation.

One of the most empowering aspects of the Psalms is their ability to validate and articulate emotions that are often suppressed or dismissed in women's experiences. The Psalms of lament, such as Psalm 13 and Psalm 22, create space for expressing anger, sorrow, and frustration, emotions that are too often labeled as unworthy or inappropriate in patriarchal religious contexts. Women reading these Psalms can find a spiritual mirror for their struggles, a reminder that their voices and emotions are not only valid but sacred. The ability to name pain and demand change is a deeply empowering act, one that reclaims the right to confront injustice and seek transformation.

The Psalms also provide a pathway for connecting personal faith with collective action. Texts like Psalm 137, which reflects on the grief and resilience of a community in exile, invite women to see their struggles as part of a larger narrative of resistance and hope. These prayers remind women that they are not alone in their journeys; they are part of a tradition that has long sought justice and liberation. By praying and meditating on these texts, women can draw strength from this collective history, finding solidarity with others who have turned their faith into a source of action and advocacy.

Furthermore, the Psalms inspire women to see themselves as active participants in the work of justice. Psalm 23, often read as a source of comfort, can also be a call to courage: "Even though I walk through the darkest valley, I will fear no evil, for you are with me." For women facing personal or systemic challenges, these words affirm the presence of divine strength, encouraging them to act boldly in the face of fear. Whether advocating for equality, leading community initiatives, or mentoring others, women can draw on the Psalms as a spiritual foundation for their leadership and activism.

The transformative potential of the Psalms extends beyond individual empowerment to community-building. Women gathering to pray or reflect on the Psalms together create spaces where their voices are heard and their experiences honored. These collective practices foster solidarity, deepening relationships and building networks of support that sustain movements for change. The communal nature of the Psalms reminds women that their strength is magnified when shared, that their prayers and actions are more powerful when joined with others.

Empowered by the Psalms, women can mobilize action that reflects both spiritual depth and practical engagement. By reclaiming these texts as tools for resistance and renewal, they challenge the narratives that have sought to confine them and affirm their role as leaders in faith and justice. The Psalms, alive with the cries and hopes of generations, continue to inspire courage, solidarity, and transformation, offering women a profound resource for spiritual empowerment and collective action.

The Book of Exodus - Liberation Theology for Women Exodus as a Narrative of Liberation

The story of the Israelites' exodus from Egypt stands as one of the most powerful narratives of liberation in scripture. It is a story of a people who, bound by oppression and dehumanized by systemic injustice, rise up to claim their freedom with the help of divine intervention. For centuries, the Exodus has inspired countless movements for justice, offering a template for resistance, resilience, and hope in the face of oppression. For women, this narrative resonates deeply as a metaphor for their own struggles for freedom from patriarchal systems that have sought to confine, control, and silence them. By engaging with the Exodus story through the lens of liberation theology, women can find a source of empowerment and a roadmap for collective resistance and transformation.

The Exodus begins in the land of Egypt, where the Israelites are enslaved under Pharaoh's rule, forced into labor, and stripped of their autonomy and humanity. This context mirrors the lived experiences of women who face systemic oppression, whether through legal restrictions, cultural expectations, or interpersonal dynamics that limit their freedom and agency. Like the Israelites, women often find themselves bound by structures designed to maintain control and suppress dissent. These parallels make the story of the Exodus particularly poignant for women, as it speaks to the pain of dehumanization while affirming the possibility of liberation.

The role of women in the Exodus narrative is particularly striking. Before Moses ever confronts Pharaoh, it is the courage of women that sets the stage for liberation. The midwives Shiphrah and Puah defy Pharaoh's command to kill Hebrew baby boys, choosing instead to preserve life and resist injustice (Exodus 1:15–21). Their actions demonstrate the power of quiet, strategic resistance, an act of faith and defiance that challenges the systemic violence of their time. Likewise, Moses' mother and sister play pivotal roles in protecting him, ensuring his survival and eventual leadership. These women are not passive bystanders; they are active agents of change whose courage and ingenuity lay the foundation for the deliverance of their people.

As the narrative unfolds, the Exodus becomes a story not only of liberation but also of identity and covenant. The Israelites' journey out of Egypt is marked by moments of doubt, struggle, and growth, reflecting the complexities of any movement toward freedom. For women, these themes resonate in the ongoing struggle to dismantle patriarchal systems and build lives defined by agency and equality. The story acknowledges that liberation is not instantaneous or easy, it is a process that requires courage, perseverance, and faith in the possibility of transformation.

The divine role in the Exodus also offers a powerful framework for women's liberation theology. God is not a distant observer but an active participant in the Israelites' journey, hearing their cries and intervening on their behalf. This vision of a God who stands with the oppressed challenges the patriarchal interpretations of scripture that portray God as aligned with systems of control and hierarchy. Instead, the Exodus reveals a God committed to justice, liberation, and the flourishing of all people. For women, this image of the divine affirms their worth and their right to freedom, challenging the theological justifications used to perpetuate inequality.

The story of the Exodus is not just a tale of ancient deliverance; it is a living narrative that continues to inspire resistance and hope. For women, it serves as a reminder that liberation is both a spiritual and collective journey, one that requires courage, faith, and the willingness to challenge systems of oppression. By engaging with the Exodus through the lens of their own struggles, women can find strength and inspiration to rise up, claim their freedom, and envision a world where justice and equality prevail.

The Role of Women in Exodus

The book of Exodus is often remembered as the story of Moses and
the Israelites' journey from slavery to freedom, but this traditional
narrative frequently overlooks the vital roles played by women in the
liberation process. From the courage of the midwives Shiphrah and
Puah to the leadership of Miriam, women are central to the Exodus
story, actively shaping its outcomes and embodying the values of
resistance, faith, and justice. Their contributions challenge patriarchal
interpretations that minimize or erase women's roles, offering a fuller
and more inclusive understanding of the narrative.

Miriam, the sister of Moses and Aaron, emerges as a significant figure
in the Exodus story, both in her actions and in her leadership. Early
in the narrative, Miriam plays a critical role in preserving Moses' life.
As Pharaoh's decree demands the death of all Hebrew baby boys,
Moses' mother places him in a basket on the Nile, entrusting his fate
to divine protection. Miriam watches over her brother and cleverly
intervenes when Pharaoh's daughter discovers him, ensuring that
Moses is cared for by their mother (Exodus 2:1–10). This act of
bravery and resourcefulness not only saves Moses but sets the stage for
his eventual leadership and the liberation of the Israelites.

Miriam's role does not end there. After the Israelites cross the Red
Sea, escaping the pursuing Egyptian army, Miriam leads the women
in a song of celebration and triumph. "Then Miriam the prophet,
Aaron's sister, took a tambourine in her hand, and all the women
followed her, with tambourines and dancing. Miriam sang to them:
'Sing to the Lord, for he is highly exalted. Both horse and driver he
has hurled into the sea'" (Exodus 15:20–21). Her designation as a
prophet underscores her spiritual authority and her leadership within
the community. Miriam's song, one of the earliest recorded in
scripture, is an expression of collective liberation, affirming the central
role of women in both the spiritual and cultural life of the Israelites.

The courage and leadership of other women in Exodus also challenge
traditional narratives that marginalize women's contributions.
Shiphrah and Puah, the Hebrew midwives, defy Pharaoh's orders to
kill male infants, risking their lives to preserve the future of their
people (Exodus 1:15–21). Their actions represent a powerful example
of civil disobedience grounded in faith and moral conviction. These

women are among the first in the Exodus story to confront the injustice of Pharaoh's rule, setting the tone for the larger narrative of resistance.

Additionally, Moses' mother and Pharaoh's daughter each play critical roles in ensuring his survival. Moses' mother demonstrates both creativity and courage in hiding her son and placing him in the basket, while Pharaoh's daughter defies her father's decree by adopting and raising Moses as her own. These acts of defiance and compassion underscore the importance of women's agency in the story, highlighting their role as protectors and enablers of liberation.

The traditional focus on Moses as the singular hero of the Exodus often obscures these women's contributions, perpetuating a narrative that aligns leadership and agency exclusively with men. Reexamining the role of women in Exodus not only restores their rightful place in the story but also challenges patriarchal assumptions that have shaped interpretations of scripture. By recognizing figures like Miriam, Shiphrah, and Puah as central to the narrative, we gain a more nuanced and inclusive understanding of the Exodus as a collective journey toward liberation.

For contemporary readers, these women offer powerful examples of courage, leadership, and resistance. Their stories inspire us to recognize the often-overlooked contributions of women in movements for justice and to honor the ways in which women continue to lead and shape the fight for liberation in the world today.

## Modern Parallels

The Israelites' journey from slavery to freedom in the book of Exodus serves as a powerful metaphor for contemporary women's struggles to break free from systemic oppression. Just as the Israelites faced the dehumanizing structures of Pharaoh's empire, modern women contend with deeply entrenched systems of patriarchy, inequality, and control that limit their freedom and agency. By drawing parallels between the ancient narrative and today's fight for justice, we can uncover timeless lessons of resilience, solidarity, and faith in the possibility of transformation.

The oppression of the Israelites under Pharaoh mirrors the systemic challenges women face in the modern world. Pharaoh's regime relied on the forced labor of the Israelites to build his empire, exploiting their bodies and denying their humanity. Similarly, patriarchal systems continue to exploit women's labor, often undervaluing their contributions in both the formal workforce and unpaid domestic roles. Wage gaps, gender-based violence, reproductive restrictions, and workplace discrimination are contemporary manifestations of the same dehumanizing forces that sought to suppress the Israelites. Women, like the Israelites, are often denied autonomy and expected to conform to societal structures that prioritize the interests of the powerful over their freedom and dignity.

The journey of the Israelites also highlights the collective nature of liberation, a theme that resonates deeply with modern movements for women's rights. The Exodus was not the story of one person's emancipation but of an entire people rising up to claim their freedom. Similarly, the fight for women's liberation is not an individual endeavor but a collective struggle that requires solidarity across boundaries of race, class, and geography. Movements like #MeToo, women's marches, and grassroots activism echo the communal resilience of the Israelites, demonstrating the strength that emerges when women unite to confront oppression and demand change.

The role of leadership in the Exodus narrative finds modern parallels in the women who lead today's movements for justice. Figures like Miriam, Shiphrah, and Puah remind us of the importance of courage, creativity, and moral conviction in challenging systems of power. In contemporary contexts, women leaders are at the forefront of fights for reproductive rights, gender equality, and racial justice, often at great personal risk. Like the midwives who defied Pharaoh's orders, these leaders confront laws, norms, and policies designed to maintain control, embodying the same spirit of resistance and faith that drives the Exodus story.

The Israelites' wilderness journey also reflects the ongoing nature of the fight for liberation. Freedom from Pharaoh's grip did not immediately lead to a life of ease; the Israelites faced years of struggle, doubt, and growth as they forged their identity as a liberated people. This process mirrors the modern fight for women's rights, which is often met with setbacks, resistance, and the slow dismantling of deeply ingrained systems. The wilderness journey reminds us that liberation is not an endpoint but an ongoing process, requiring perseverance, collective action, and faith in the possibility of a better future.

The divine role in the Exodus narrative offers a source of inspiration for women's struggles today. God's active presence in hearing the cries of the Israelites, intervening on their behalf, and guiding them toward freedom reflects a commitment to justice that transcends time. For women fighting against oppression, this image of a liberating God affirms the sacredness of their struggle and the hope that justice, though delayed, is inevitable. It challenges patriarchal interpretations of scripture that portray God as aligned with systems of control, instead presenting a vision of the divine as a force for liberation and transformation.

Drawing these parallels between the Exodus and contemporary women's struggles underscores the enduring relevance of this ancient story. It invites women to see their fight for freedom not as an isolated effort but as part of a larger, sacred narrative of resistance and redemption. Like the Israelites, women today are forging a path toward liberation, confronting the pharaohs of their time with courage, resilience, and a vision of a world where justice and equality prevail.

Lessons for Resistance

The story of the Exodus, rich with themes of perseverance, faith, and collective action, offers timeless lessons for modern liberation movements. The journey of the Israelites from bondage to freedom serves as a blueprint for resistance, demonstrating how oppressed communities can confront systemic injustice, sustain hope in the face of adversity, and build solidarity as they move toward liberation. For contemporary movements, these themes provide both inspiration and practical guidance, illuminating a path for those who dare to challenge entrenched systems of power.

One of the most striking lessons of the Exodus is the importance of perseverance. The Israelites' journey to freedom was not a straightforward or swift process; it was marked by repeated setbacks, moments of doubt, and grueling trials in the wilderness. Yet, despite the enormity of the challenges they faced, the Israelites pressed forward, sustained by the promise of liberation and the hope of a better future. For modern movements, perseverance is equally critical. The fight for justice and equality is rarely linear or easy. It demands a long-term commitment to the cause, even in the face of resistance, disillusionment, or apparent failure. The Israelites' story reminds us that liberation is a process, not an event, and that enduring the wilderness is an integral part of the journey.

Faith is another central theme of the Exodus, not only in the divine but also in the power of a shared vision. The Israelites cried out to God for deliverance, trusting that their suffering was seen and that justice would come. This faith was not passive; it was an active force that propelled them to take bold steps, following Moses and challenging Pharaoh's oppression. For contemporary liberation movements, faith can take many forms, faith in the power of collective action, in the resilience of the human spirit, or in the possibility of systemic change. It is the belief that injustice is neither permanent nor invincible and that a better world is not only possible but worth fighting for. This conviction sustains movements in their darkest moments, providing the courage to persist even when victory feels distant.

The theme of collective action in the Exodus narrative offers a powerful model for modern movements. The liberation of the

Israelites was not the work of one person but of an entire community united by a shared goal. While Moses often takes center stage, the story is replete with examples of collective resistance, from the defiance of the Hebrew midwives Shiphrah and Puah to the communal courage of the Israelites crossing the Red Sea. This emphasis on solidarity is a crucial lesson for today's movements, where success often depends on the ability to build coalitions, amplify diverse voices, and work together toward common objectives. The Exodus narrative teaches that true liberation cannot be achieved in isolation; it requires the collective strength, wisdom, and participation of the whole community.

For modern movements, these lessons offer a roadmap for confronting oppression and advancing justice. Perseverance reminds us to stay the course, even when progress seems slow or setbacks arise. Faith inspires hope and resilience, affirming that the struggle is meaningful and that change is possible. Collective action underscores the necessity of solidarity, emphasizing that liberation is a shared endeavor that requires the contributions and leadership of many. These themes, woven together, provide the foundation for resistance that is both strategic and transformative.

The story of the Exodus is not merely a historical account but a living narrative that continues to inspire and guide those who seek freedom from oppression. By extracting its lessons of perseverance, faith, and collective action, modern movements can draw strength from its wisdom and find a blueprint for their own struggles. Just as the Israelites forged a path through the wilderness, contemporary communities can navigate their own journeys toward justice, empowered by the enduring truths of this sacred story.

The Gospels Reimagined - Jesus, the Radical Ally Reframing Christ

The Gospels present Jesus not as a passive figure upholding the societal norms of his time but as a radical disruptor of oppressive systems, including the deeply ingrained patriarchy of his era. Through his words and actions, Jesus repeatedly challenged cultural and religious conventions that marginalized women and other vulnerable groups, offering instead a vision of community rooted in justice, dignity, and inclusivity. Reframing Christ as a radical ally to the marginalized reveals the transformative potential of the Gospels, inspiring contemporary readers to follow his example in resisting systems of oppression and uplifting those who are most excluded.

From the outset of his ministry, Jesus defied expectations by centering those who were pushed to the edges of society. His interactions with women, in particular, stand out as acts of radical inclusion in a culture that often devalued their voices and agency. While the religious and social norms of the time relegated women to subordinate roles, Jesus treated them as equals, affirming their dignity and involving them in his mission. The Samaritan woman at the well (John 4:1–26) exemplifies this revolutionary approach. In speaking with her, Jesus broke multiple taboos: he addressed a woman publicly, engaged with a Samaritan (a group despised by Jews), and acknowledged her complex personal history without judgment. Their conversation is the longest recorded dialogue between Jesus and any individual in the Gospels, culminating in the woman becoming a witness and evangelist to her community. This interaction underscores Jesus' willingness to see beyond societal labels and recognize the full humanity and potential of marginalized individuals.

Jesus' relationships with women extended beyond isolated encounters to include their active participation in his ministry. Women like Mary Magdalene, Joanna, and Susanna traveled with Jesus and supported his mission (Luke 8:1–3). Mary of Bethany sat at Jesus' feet to learn from him, a position traditionally reserved for male disciples (Luke 10:38–42). When Martha, her sister, expressed concern about Mary's unconventional behavior, Jesus affirmed Mary's choice, stating, "Mary has chosen what is better, and it will not be taken away from her." This affirmation of a woman's right to theological learning and spiritual engagement directly challenged the cultural norms that restricted women's access to religious instruction and leadership.

Perhaps most striking is Jesus' consistent elevation of women as examples of faith and devotion. In Mark 5:25–34, he heals a woman suffering from chronic bleeding, a condition that would have rendered her ritually unclean and socially ostracized. Far from shunning her, Jesus commends her faith, addressing her as "daughter" and restoring her place in the community. Similarly, he defends the woman who anoints him with costly perfume, recognizing her act as one of profound spiritual significance (Mark 14:3–9). These moments highlight Jesus' rejection of purity laws and social stigmas that dehumanized women, offering instead a vision of inclusion and grace.

Jesus' actions also extended to other marginalized groups, including the poor, the sick, and the socially outcast. He openly associated with tax collectors, lepers, and sinners, challenging the religious authorities who sought to maintain rigid boundaries of purity and exclusion. His teachings consistently emphasized the reversal of societal hierarchies: "The last will be first, and the first will be last" (Matthew 20:16). This radical reimagining of power and status destabilized the patriarchal and class-based systems of his time, offering a glimpse of a kingdom where all are valued equally.

Reframing Christ as a disruptor of patriarchal norms reveals the revolutionary heart of the Gospel message. His interactions with women and other marginalized groups were not incidental but central to his mission, demonstrating a commitment to justice, equality, and the restoration of human dignity. For contemporary readers, this image of Jesus as a radical ally challenges us to embody his example, confronting the systems that oppress and building communities that reflect the inclusive love and justice of God's kingdom.

Women in the Gospels

The Gospels are filled with stories of women whose lives are transformed through their encounters with Jesus. These narratives stand out as profound examples of empowerment in a cultural context that often silenced and marginalized women. By engaging directly with these women and affirming their dignity and worth, Jesus dismantled the societal and religious norms that sought to constrain them. Stories like the Samaritan woman at the well and the woman caught in adultery showcase Christ's commitment to justice, inclusion, and liberation, offering a powerful vision of what it means to uplift and empower the marginalized.

The story of the Samaritan woman at the well, found in John 4:1–26, is remarkable for its depth and significance. Jesus, a Jewish man, speaks publicly with a Samaritan woman, an interaction that defied multiple cultural taboos. Jews and Samaritans shared a long history of animosity, and women were often excluded from public theological discussions. Yet, Jesus not only engages with this woman but also initiates the conversation, asking her for water and offering her "living water" in return. In doing so, he transcends societal boundaries, treating her as an equal participant in a dialogue about faith and worship.

As their conversation unfolds, Jesus acknowledges the woman's personal history, including her relationships, without judgment or condemnation. Instead of defining her by societal stigmas, he sees her potential and entrusts her with the revelation of his identity as the Messiah. Empowered by this encounter, the woman becomes a witness to her community, sharing the news of Jesus and leading others to him. Her transformation from an outsider to a central figure in her community's spiritual awakening highlights the power of Christ's actions to restore dignity and agency to those marginalized by society.

The story of the woman caught in adultery, recounted in John 8:1–11, further underscores Jesus' radical empowerment of women. Brought before Jesus by religious leaders eager to test him, this woman is publicly shamed and threatened with death by stoning. The situation is steeped in injustice, as the woman is singled out while her male counterpart is notably absent, a reflection of the double standards and patriarchal practices of the time. Rather than succumbing to the leaders' trap, Jesus disrupts their plans with a simple yet profound challenge: "Let any one of you who is without sin be the first to throw a stone at her."

This statement not only exposes the hypocrisy of the accusers but also shifts the focus from the woman's alleged guilt to the broader issue of systemic injustice. As the crowd disperses, Jesus turns to the woman and says, "Neither do I condemn you. Go now and leave your life of sin." These words are not a dismissal of moral responsibility but an affirmation of her humanity and an invitation to a new beginning. Jesus refuses to reduce her to a symbol of sin or shame, instead empowering her to reclaim her life on her terms.

In both stories, Jesus challenges the social and religious norms that sought to marginalize and dehumanize women. By engaging with them directly, affirming their worth, and entrusting them with responsibility, he transforms their lives and redefines their roles within their communities. These narratives demonstrate that empowerment is not about imposing control but about restoring agency and affirming the inherent dignity of every individual.

For contemporary readers, these stories invite reflection on the ways in which women's voices and experiences are still marginalized in religious and societal contexts. They challenge us to follow Christ's example, creating spaces where women are valued, empowered, and fully included in the work of justice and faith. In reclaiming these stories, we reclaim the Gospel's liberatory message, affirming the sacredness of every life and the transformative power of inclusion and love.

Jesus' Advocacy for Women

Jesus' interactions with women throughout the Gospels stand as radical affirmations of their dignity and worth in a society that often marginalized and devalued them. His actions and teachings challenged deeply ingrained societal norms, disrupting the patriarchal structures that confined women to subordinate roles. By engaging with women as equals, uplifting their voices, and defending their humanity, Christ exemplified a vision of justice and inclusion that remains revolutionary. His advocacy for women reveals a Gospel message rooted in the restoration of human dignity and the rejection of oppressive systems.

One of the most striking ways Jesus affirmed women's worth was by engaging with them publicly and directly, a profound departure from the cultural norms of his time. In a society where women were often excluded from theological discussions and their testimonies dismissed, Jesus not only spoke with women but treated them as equal participants in spiritual conversations. The Samaritan woman at the well (John 4:1–26) exemplifies this approach. By addressing her openly and discussing matters of profound theological significance, Jesus acknowledged her spiritual agency and intelligence. This act not only affirmed her value but also broke down barriers of gender, ethnicity, and social stigma, challenging the discriminatory practices of his day.

Jesus' advocacy extended beyond dialogue to include acts of healing and restoration that defied societal expectations. In Mark 5:25–34, he heals a woman suffering from chronic bleeding, a condition that rendered her ritually unclean and ostracized from her community. Rather than recoiling from her touch, as the norms of ritual purity would dictate, Jesus affirms her faith and addresses her as "daughter," a term of profound respect and care. His response not only restores her health but also reintegrates her into her community, affirming her humanity and dignity in the process.

Similarly, in Luke 13:10–17, Jesus heals a woman who had been crippled for 18 years, doing so in the synagogue on the Sabbath. When criticized by religious leaders for breaking Sabbath laws, Jesus defends the woman, calling her a "daughter of Abraham." This designation is significant, as it places her on equal footing with men in the covenantal relationship with God, a radical assertion in a culture that often relegated women to the margins of religious life. Through this act, Jesus not only heals her physical ailment but also challenges the legalism and exclusionary practices that devalued women.

Perhaps most powerfully, Jesus advocates for women by rejecting the punitive and hypocritical double standards of his society. The story of the woman caught in adultery (John 8:1–11) reveals his commitment to justice and mercy. When the woman is brought before him to be stoned, Jesus exposes the hypocrisy of her accusers, who fail to bring her male counterpart to account. His challenge, "Let any one of you who is without sin be the first to throw a stone," shifts the focus from the woman's alleged guilt to the unjust practices of her accusers. By refusing to condemn her, Jesus restores her dignity and offers her the opportunity for a new beginning, affirming her humanity over societal judgment.

In all these interactions, Jesus consistently elevates women's worth, rejecting the cultural and religious norms that sought to silence or diminish them. His actions demonstrate that true advocacy requires more than words; it demands confronting oppressive systems, amplifying marginalized voices, and restoring the dignity of those who have been dehumanized. For contemporary readers, Jesus' advocacy for women serves as a model for challenging gender inequality and building communities that reflect the radical inclusivity of the Gospel. His example calls us to affirm the worth of all people and to work tirelessly for a world where justice and dignity prevail.

## Modern Implications

Positioning Jesus as an ally in today's feminist movements offers a powerful model for disrupting systems of oppression and advancing gender justice. Through his actions, teachings, and radical inclusivity, Jesus demonstrated a commitment to challenging societal norms that devalued women and marginalized groups. By reframing his example in the context of modern struggles, feminist movements can draw on his life and message as a source of inspiration, courage, and solidarity in the fight for equality.

In the Gospels, Jesus consistently aligned himself with those who were dehumanized or excluded, including women, the poor, and the socially stigmatized. His interactions with women—whether affirming the faith of the woman with chronic bleeding, defending the woman caught in adultery, or empowering the Samaritan woman to become a witness to her community, demonstrate his rejection of patriarchal norms. In a world where women's voices were often dismissed and their roles confined to the private sphere, Jesus treated women as full participants in spiritual and communal life. This radical inclusivity, a hallmark of his ministry, offers a profound critique of contemporary systems that perpetuate gender inequality and a roadmap for disrupting those systems.

Modern feminist movements share this commitment to challenging oppressive structures and amplifying marginalized voices. Like Jesus, these movements seek to dismantle hierarchies that privilege power over justice and domination over equity. Positioning Christ as an ally in this work highlights the compatibility of feminist principles with the liberatory message of the Gospel. His example provides a theological foundation for confronting the sexism, misogyny, and systemic inequalities that continue to plague societies today.

One of the most significant implications of viewing Jesus as an ally in feminist movements is his emphasis on the dignity and worth of every individual, particularly those devalued by societal norms. Feminism often grapples with issues of intersectionality, recognizing that oppression does not operate in a vacuum but intersects with race, class, sexuality, and other identities. Jesus' actions in the Gospels reflect an awareness of these overlapping struggles. His willingness to engage with a Samaritan woman, someone marginalized not only by her gender but also by her ethnicity, offers a model for addressing the complexities of intersecting oppressions in feminist activism. By centering those most impacted by injustice, Jesus' example calls us to build movements that are inclusive, intersectional, and deeply rooted in the pursuit of justice for all.

Jesus' approach to power also offers critical insights for modern feminist movements. He consistently subverted traditional power structures, rejecting domination and control in favor of service and humility. His teachings on leadership, "Whoever wants to become great among you must be your servant," (Matthew 20:26)—challenge the hierarchical systems that underpin patriarchy. For feminists, this model of servant leadership underscores the importance of creating collaborative and equitable structures that prioritize the collective over individual power. It invites activists to reimagine leadership as an act of service to the broader community, reflecting the values of compassion and justice.

Moreover, Jesus' unwavering commitment to truth-telling and accountability resonates deeply with feminist advocacy. He confronted religious and political authorities, exposing their hypocrisy and challenging their exploitation of the vulnerable. This courage to speak out against injustice, even at great personal cost, mirrors the bravery of feminist leaders who confront sexism, misogyny, and systemic violence in their fight for equality. By following Christ's example, modern movements can draw strength from the knowledge that disrupting oppression is both a moral imperative and a sacred calling.

Positioning Jesus as an ally in feminist movements reminds us that faith and justice are not mutually exclusive but deeply interconnected. His life and teachings offer a model for resisting oppression, amplifying marginalized voices, and building communities grounded in love and equality. For feminists seeking to disrupt patriarchal systems and create a more just world, Christ's example provides both inspiration and a profound affirmation of the work they undertake.

Reimagining Parables

Reimagining the parables of Jesus through a feminist lens reveals their profound potential to inspire justice, inclusion, and empowerment. These short but powerful stories were designed to challenge conventional thinking and illuminate the radical values of God's kingdom, a realm where hierarchies are overturned, the marginalized are centered, and power is redefined. When viewed through a feminist lens, the parables speak directly to the struggles and aspirations of women, offering a vision of equity and liberation that challenges patriarchal norms and affirms the dignity of all.

One striking example is the parable of the Good Samaritan (Luke 10:25–37). Traditionally understood as a call to compassion and neighborly love, this parable gains new depth when reimagined through a feminist lens. In the story, the Samaritan, a member of a despised and marginalized group, becomes the hero, crossing boundaries of ethnicity and social status to care for a wounded stranger. This narrative invites us to reflect on the ways in which women, often excluded or devalued by patriarchal systems, embody the radical love and solidarity that Jesus praises. It challenges us to recognize and honor the caregiving roles women frequently undertake in societies that fail to value their contributions. At the same time, the story calls for a reordering of power structures, asking us to see those dismissed by the world as central to the work of justice and compassion.

The parable of the Persistent Widow (Luke 18:1–8) offers another rich opportunity for feminist reinterpretation. In this story, a widow, one of the most vulnerable figures in the ancient world, relentlessly seeks justice from an indifferent judge. Her persistence ultimately compels the judge to act, making her a symbol of unwavering faith and resilience. Viewed through a feminist lens, this parable affirms the power of women's voices and the necessity of challenging unjust systems, even when those in power are resistant or dismissive. The widow's determination embodies the struggles of women who fight for their rights and the rights of others, often in the face of systemic oppression. Her victory underscores the transformative potential of persistence, solidarity, and the refusal to accept injustice as inevitable.

The parable of the Mustard Seed (Matthew 13:31–32) also resonates deeply when reimagined with feminist values in mind. This story, which describes how a tiny seed grows into a tree that provides shelter for birds, speaks to the power of small beginnings and seemingly insignificant acts. In a patriarchal context where women's contributions are often overlooked or undervalued, this parable affirms the profound impact of everyday actions and hidden labor. It reminds us that transformative change often starts in the margins, in spaces and acts deemed insignificant by those in power. Reinterpreted through a feminist lens, the mustard seed becomes a metaphor for the quiet yet revolutionary work of women who nurture communities, challenge norms, and build foundations for a more equitable world.

Reimagining parables through this lens also involves reclaiming the figures and imagery within them as symbols of inclusion and empowerment. The woman in the parable of the Lost Coin (Luke 15:8–10), for instance, becomes a model of relentless care and value, demonstrating the worth of every individual, particularly those who have been ignored or discarded. Her joy upon finding the lost coin reflects the transformative power of recognition and restoration, themes central to feminist advocacy for the marginalized and oppressed.

These feminist reinterpretations of the parables affirm their enduring relevance and liberatory potential. By centering justice, inclusion, and empowerment, they challenge the patriarchal readings that have too often distorted their meanings. They invite us to see the parables not as moralistic tales but as revolutionary visions of a world where the last are first, the overlooked are celebrated, and justice flows like a river. For women and all who seek liberation, the parables offer a powerful spiritual and ethical framework for building a more just and inclusive future.

Building a New Narrative

Reclaiming the Gospels as tools for radical love and systemic change is an urgent and transformative act. For too long, these sacred texts have been confined to interpretations that emphasize personal morality while ignoring or justifying systemic oppression. Yet, at their core, the Gospels are revolutionary documents, stories of a Christ who disrupted societal norms, challenged entrenched power structures, and uplifted the marginalized. By reclaiming this narrative, readers are invited to embrace a faith that is not static or passive but dynamic and active, rooted in love and committed to justice. This is not about rewriting scripture but rediscovering its radical heart and using it to inspire change in our world.

The life and teachings of Jesus exemplify a profound commitment to systemic change. His ministry was not confined to private, spiritual matters but extended to the public and political realms, where he confronted the religious, economic, and social injustices of his time. He healed the sick, fed the hungry, and broke bread with outcasts, not as isolated acts of charity but as declarations of a new order where every person's dignity is affirmed. When he overturned the tables of the money changers in the temple (Matthew 21:12–13), he directly challenged the exploitation embedded in religious and economic systems. His parables consistently highlighted the inequities of the world, calling listeners to imagine and work toward a kingdom where the last are first and the forgotten are celebrated.

Reclaiming the Gospels begins with recognizing these themes of radical love and justice as central to Jesus' message. This requires moving beyond interpretations that reduce the Gospels to personal salvation or individual piety. While these aspects of faith are important, they are incomplete without a recognition of Jesus' broader mission to transform society. His teachings are deeply political, addressing issues of power, inequality, and community. Reclaiming the Gospels means reclaiming their call to action, a call to confront systems of oppression, advocate for the marginalized, and create a world that reflects the inclusive love of God.

For women and other marginalized groups, reclaiming the Gospels is especially empowering. Jesus consistently elevated the voices and experiences of those overlooked or silenced by society. He affirmed the Samaritan woman at the well as a theologian and witness, defended the woman caught in adultery from condemnation, and celebrated the persistence of the widow seeking justice. These stories challenge patriarchal and exclusionary readings of scripture, offering a vision of a Christ who sees, values, and empowers the marginalized. By reclaiming these narratives, readers can challenge the systems that continue to oppress and silence women and others today.

Reclaiming the Gospels also involves embracing their capacity to inspire collective action. Jesus' vision of the kingdom of God was not an individualistic or distant ideal but a communal reality to be lived and built in the here and now. His followers were not isolated believers but a movement, united by a shared commitment to love, justice, and inclusion. Today, reclaiming the Gospels calls us to build communities that reflect these values, spaces where diversity is celebrated, solidarity is practiced, and justice is pursued relentlessly.

This new narrative, rooted in the radical love of Christ, demands courage and imagination. It challenges us to confront our own complicity in systems of oppression, to dismantle harmful structures, and to build alternatives that reflect the transformative power of the Gospel. It is a call to live out our faith in ways that disrupt injustice and embody love, not as abstract ideals but as lived realities.

The Gospels, reclaimed as tools for systemic change, become more than ancient texts; they become blueprints for a better world. They remind us that the work of justice is sacred, that love is revolutionary, and that faith, when lived boldly, can transform not only individuals but entire societies. This is the narrative we are called to reclaim and live, a narrative of hope, courage, and radical transformation.

Revelations of Revolution - A Blueprint for Dismantling Oppression
Revelation as a Text of Resistance

The book of Revelation, often misunderstood as a cryptic prophecy of
doom and destruction, is, at its core, a powerful text of resistance and
hope. Written during a time of intense persecution and oppression,
Revelation speaks to a community struggling to maintain faith in the
face of empire and systemic injustice. Its vivid apocalyptic imagery,
beasts, dragons, and celestial battles, has been interpreted through
fear and sensationalism, but a closer reading reveals its true purpose:
to inspire courage and perseverance by envisioning the dismantling of
oppressive systems and the triumph of justice. Reframing Revelation
through this lens transforms it from a text of despair into a blueprint
for revolutionary hope and liberation.

The historical context of Revelation is crucial to understanding its
message. Written by John of Patmos, likely during the reign of the
Roman Emperor Domitian, the text reflects the realities of a
community living under the shadow of imperial power. Rome's
dominance was not merely political but cultural and religious,
demanding allegiance to the emperor as a divine figure. For early
Christians, this posed a profound challenge to their faith and identity.
Revelation uses apocalyptic imagery not to predict the end of the
world but to unveil ("apocalypse" means "unveiling") the true nature
of empire as corrupt and unsustainable. It is a call to resistance,
urging believers to remain steadfast in their commitment to justice
and faith, even in the face of overwhelming power.

The symbolic language of Revelation, often misconstrued as literal
prediction, serves as a critique of systemic oppression. The "beast"
that rises from the sea (Revelation 13:1) is a representation of empire,
its voracious appetite for power, its exploitation of resources, and its
dehumanization of those under its rule. The "great harlot" Babylon
(Revelation 17:1–6), drunk on the blood of the saints, symbolizes the
corrupt economic and political systems that prioritize wealth and
power over human dignity. These images are not forecasts of future
calamities but searing indictments of the structures of domination that
perpetuate injustice. For those living under such systems, these visions
expose the truth of their oppression and offer hope for its eventual
dismantling.

Revelation's message of resistance is underscored by its imagery of ultimate justice. The heavenly city of New Jerusalem (Revelation 21:1–4) represents a vision of a world made whole, where God's justice and love reign supreme. This is not an escapist fantasy but a counter-narrative to the empire's claims of invincibility. By imagining a reality where oppression is no more and every tear is wiped away, Revelation offers a revolutionary vision of hope that empowers communities to resist domination and work toward liberation. It assures its readers that the powers of oppression, no matter how mighty they seem, are not eternal and will ultimately fall.

For modern readers, reframing Revelation as a text of resistance has profound implications. Its apocalyptic imagery challenges us to confront the "beasts" and "Babylons" of our own time, systems of patriarchy, racism, economic exploitation, and environmental degradation. It invites us to see through the illusions of power and privilege, exposing their violence and unsustainability. Revelation calls us not to passivity but to active engagement in the work of dismantling oppression and building communities of justice, love, and equity.

By reclaiming Revelation as a text of resistance, we move beyond fear and fatalism to embrace its transformative vision of hope. It is a reminder that faith is not a retreat from the world's struggles but a source of strength to confront them. Revelation challenges us to imagine a better world and to take bold steps toward making that vision a reality, trusting that justice, not oppression, will have the final word.

Patriarchal Misuse of Revelation

The book of Revelation, with its vivid apocalyptic imagery and cryptic symbolism, has long been one of the most misinterpreted texts in the Bible. While it was originally written as a message of resistance and hope for communities facing oppression under Roman imperial rule, patriarchal and institutional forces have frequently weaponized Revelation to instill fear, maintain control, and suppress transformative action. This misuse has distorted its liberatory essence, transforming it from a text of justice and renewal into one of fearmongering and submission.

One of the primary ways Revelation has been weaponized is through its apocalyptic imagery, which has been stripped of its historical and symbolic context. Passages describing the beast, the dragon, and the judgments of God have been recast as literal prophecies of impending doom, used to terrify believers into compliance. This approach shifts the focus from systemic critique to personal fear, making Revelation a tool for control rather than liberation. By framing the text as a prediction of catastrophic events or eternal damnation, patriarchal systems divert attention away from its call to resist oppression and dismantle unjust structures.

This fear-based interpretation often aligns with patriarchal power dynamics, reinforcing hierarchies and silencing dissent. Religious authorities have historically used Revelation's imagery to enforce conformity, particularly around gender roles and obedience. The portrayal of Babylon as the "great harlot" (Revelation 17) has been misused to shame and control women, equating their autonomy or deviation from prescribed norms with moral corruption. Such interpretations reduce Babylon's symbolism, a critique of corrupt empires and economic exploitation, to a simplistic condemnation of women's sexuality and independence. This distortion reinforces patriarchal control over women's bodies and choices, diverting the text's critique of systemic injustice into a tool for personal oppression.

Similarly, Revelation's depictions of divine judgment have been co-opted to support exclusionary theologies that marginalize women, LGBTQ+ individuals, and other groups deemed "sinful" by conservative religious authorities. The language of judgment and destruction is wielded as a weapon to justify discrimination, perpetuating the idea that certain groups are inherently outside the bounds of God's grace. This approach not only distorts Revelation's message but also reinforces systems of oppression, making the text complicit in the very injustices it was written to challenge.

Another misuse of Revelation lies in its alignment with political agendas that uphold patriarchal and imperial ideologies. By emphasizing the "end times" as a future event rather than a symbolic critique of systemic evil, patriarchal interpreters have shifted the focus away from addressing present injustices. This eschatological fixation often discourages activism and resistance, suggesting that believers should endure suffering passively while awaiting divine intervention. This perspective undermines the transformative potential of Revelation, reducing it to a message of resignation rather than a call to action.

In contrast, a more contextual and liberatory reading of Revelation reveals its true purpose: to inspire hope, courage, and resistance among those facing oppression. The text's vivid imagery is not a forecast of inevitable destruction but a symbolic unveiling of the injustices of empire and the promise of divine justice. Its visions of New Jerusalem (Revelation 21:1–4) offer a powerful counter-narrative to systems of domination, imagining a world where suffering and oppression are no more. By reclaiming this vision, we can confront the ways Revelation has been misused and restore its message as one of hope and transformation.

The patriarchal misuse of Revelation serves as a cautionary tale about the dangers of distorting scripture to uphold power and control. By challenging these interpretations, we open the door to reclaiming Revelation's radical call to justice and liberation. It reminds us that faith is not a tool of fear but a source of strength to confront and dismantle oppression. When read in its proper context, Revelation becomes not a weapon of fear but a vision of hope, calling us to participate in the ongoing work of creating a more just and equitable world.

Revolutionary Themes

Revelation, often viewed through the lens of apocalyptic dread, is in truth a text brimming with revolutionary themes aimed at dismantling oppressive systems and advocating for justice and equality. While its symbolism and imagery have often been co-opted to promote fear, a closer examination of its content reveals that it is, at its core, a radical call for the overthrow of corrupt powers and the establishment of a just and equitable world. The themes of justice, equality, and the overthrow of corrupt systems permeate the text, making it not a forewarning of inevitable destruction, but a profound statement of resistance, hope, and renewal.

One of the most significant revolutionary themes in Revelation is the critique of empire and its corrupting influence. The imagery of the "beast" that rises from the sea (Revelation 13:1), symbolizing the empire, embodies the destructive power of authoritarian regimes and their capacity to oppress and exploit marginalized communities. The beast, described with blasphemous titles and an insatiable desire for power, serves as a metaphor for the unchecked greed, violence, and systemic injustice of imperial systems. Through this, Revelation underscores a critical point: empire, in all its forms, is a corrupt force that must be resisted. The imagery of the beast is not only a critique of the Roman Empire of the time but is also a timeless symbol of all oppressive and unjust systems that prioritize power over human dignity.

The fall of Babylon, described in Revelation 17-18, is another powerful metaphor for the overthrow of corrupt systems. Babylon, portrayed as a city drunk on the blood of the saints and the wealth of exploitation, represents the economic and political systems built on exploitation, inequality, and oppression. Its eventual downfall is depicted in vivid, apocalyptic terms, signaling that no system of corruption is permanent. The fall of Babylon is symbolic not just of the collapse of ancient empires but of the inevitable disintegration of any unjust system that fails to prioritize justice, equity, and compassion. In this vision, Revelation presents a revolutionary hope: that the corrupt systems of today, whether they be political, economic, or social, will ultimately fall, and justice will prevail.

Revelation also provides a radical vision of equality and the establishment of a just order. The arrival of the New Jerusalem in Revelation 21 symbolizes the fulfillment of God's justice and the creation of a society where oppression, suffering, and inequality have no place. The vision of the New Jerusalem is one where the marginalized are uplifted, and the oppressed are set free. It is a city of peace, where there is no longer any division between the people of God and the oppressed. In this vision, God's reign is established on earth, bringing with it a new world order built on equality, love, and justice. The walls of the city, adorned with precious stones, represent the divine protection and inclusion of all people, no matter their social, economic, or political status.

The theme of equality is also reflected in the reversal of fortunes that is central to the apocalyptic vision of Revelation. The first shall be last, and the last shall be first (Matthew 20:16). This is echoed in the promise of the New Jerusalem, where the oppressed will be exalted, and the powerful will be brought low. In this new world, the people of God, symbolized by the saints, the martyrs, and the poor, will be vindicated, while those who have perpetuated injustice and exploitation will face judgment. This inversion of power structures serves as a radical critique of the status quo and is a call to action for those who are oppressed to resist passively and actively work toward the fulfillment of God's just vision for the world.

Finally, Revelation emphasizes the theme of perseverance in the face of oppression. The message to the seven churches in Revelation 2-3 encourages believers to remain steadfast despite persecution, promising that those who overcome will receive their reward in God's kingdom. This perseverance is not a call for passivity or resignation, but rather for active resistance against the systems that oppress. It is a call for people of faith to stand firm, to challenge injustice, and to engage in the ongoing work of transformation. Revelation's promise of justice, equality, and the eventual overthrow of corrupt systems is not an invitation to wait passively for change but a call to actively engage in the work of resistance and revolution.

A Vision for Liberation

The book of Revelation, often mischaracterized as a cryptic forecast of doom, is in reality a profound call to action—a rallying cry for creating a world rooted in justice and compassion. Written to inspire a persecuted community under Roman imperial rule, Revelation challenges oppressive systems, unveils the truth of their corruption, and offers a transformative vision of hope and liberation. Its imagery and messages are not meant to paralyze with fear but to empower believers to resist injustice and participate in building a new world where equality and love prevail.

At its heart, Revelation confronts the stark realities of systemic oppression. The vivid symbols of the beast, the dragon, and Babylon embody the destructive forces of empire, political, economic, and social systems that exploit, dehumanize, and prioritize power over people. These symbols were directly tied to the Roman Empire in John's time, but they also speak to the ongoing struggles against corruption, inequality, and exploitation in every age. By exposing the empire's true nature, Revelation invites its readers to reject complicity and recognize the urgent need for transformation. It is a text that insists the status quo is not inevitable and that systemic injustice can, and must, be dismantled.

The vision of New Jerusalem (Revelation 21:1–4) encapsulates Revelation's liberatory promise, presenting a radical alternative to the oppressive realities of empire. This new city is not a distant dream but a blueprint for a world where justice and compassion are the foundation of human community. In this city, there is no pain, mourning, or death, and God's presence dwells with the people. The imagery of its gates, always open, signifies radical inclusivity, a rejection of the hierarchies and exclusions that perpetuate inequality. The New Jerusalem is not a private salvation for the few but a collective vision of restoration for all, a society where every tear is wiped away and every person's dignity is affirmed.

Revelation's call to action is most evident in its exhortations to resist oppression and remain faithful in the face of adversity. The letters to the seven churches (Revelation 2–3) urge communities to confront the challenges of compromise, complacency, and persecution. These letters are not passive reminders of endurance but active calls to engage in the work of justice, even at great personal cost. To "overcome" is to refuse submission to systems of domination and to work toward a world that reflects God's values of equity, love, and compassion. This message resonates profoundly in contemporary struggles for justice, reminding us that resistance is sacred and that perseverance is a necessary act of faith.

Revelation also centers the power of community in the pursuit of liberation. The text is written not to individuals but to collective bodies, emphasizing the importance of solidarity and shared action. Its vision of the saints who "washed their robes and made them white in the blood of the Lamb" (Revelation 7:14) celebrates those who have resisted oppression and remained faithful to the work of justice. This communal focus challenges the isolation often imposed by oppressive systems, offering instead a vision of unity and collective strength.

Framing Revelation as a call to action shifts the narrative from fear to empowerment. It reminds us that the apocalyptic is not about endings but unveilings, the unveiling of truth, injustice, and the possibilities for transformation. Revelation calls us to see the world as it is and to imagine it as it could be, a place where justice flows like a river and compassion binds us together. This vision is not static or distant; it is a challenge to act, to resist, and to build a world worthy of its promises. Revelation invites us all to become co-creators of this new world, trusting that the work of justice and love will ultimately triumph.

Applying Revelation Today

The book of Revelation, with its vivid imagery and symbolic narrative, provides a powerful framework for understanding and confronting contemporary struggles for gender equality. Its critique of systemic oppression, call for resistance, and vision of a new world order resonate deeply with the ongoing fight against patriarchal structures. By reinterpreting its symbolism in the context of modern struggles, Revelation can serve as a source of inspiration and empowerment for those working to dismantle gender-based injustices and build a more equitable society.

The "beast" in Revelation, a symbol of oppressive and exploitative systems (Revelation 13:1), mirrors the pervasive nature of patriarchy in today's world. Much like the beast, patriarchy operates as a global system that dehumanizes and exploits, weaving its influence into every facet of life, from economic disparities and political exclusion to cultural norms that perpetuate gender-based violence and discrimination. Revelation's depiction of the beast invites us to confront the multifaceted ways in which patriarchy asserts its power and to resist its dehumanizing grip. It challenges us to recognize that gender inequality is not a series of isolated issues but part of a larger oppressive framework that must be dismantled in its entirety.

The image of Babylon, described as a corrupt city drunk on exploitation (Revelation 17:1–6), offers another striking parallel to modern gender struggles. Babylon represents systems of unchecked greed and moral corruption, often built on the backs of the marginalized. Today, this imagery speaks to the commodification of women's bodies, the gender pay gap, and industries that profit from inequality. Patriarchal economies thrive on the exploitation of women's labor, both paid and unpaid, and on the perpetuation of harmful stereotypes that limit women's autonomy. The fall of Babylon in Revelation (Revelation 18) symbolizes the inevitable collapse of unjust systems, offering hope that these exploitative structures can and will be dismantled. It is a reminder that the fight for gender equality is part of a broader struggle for justice and that change, though challenging, is possible.

Revelation's call to perseverance and resistance speaks directly to the courage required to confront gender-based oppression. The saints who "refused to worship the beast" (Revelation 13:15) embody the resilience needed to challenge patriarchal systems that demand compliance and silence dissent. In contemporary terms, this resistance might look like advocating for policies that protect women's rights, amplifying the voices of marginalized groups, or disrupting norms that perpetuate gender inequality. Revelation's emphasis on steadfastness reminds us that the struggle for equality is not a moment but a movement, requiring sustained effort and unwavering faith in the possibility of transformation.

The vision of New Jerusalem (Revelation 21:1–4) serves as a radical counter-narrative to patriarchy's hierarchies and exclusions. This city, where "there will be no more death or mourning or crying or pain," represents a world where justice and equality prevail. Its gates, always open, symbolize radical inclusivity, a rejection of the barriers that patriarchal systems impose. For modern feminists, New Jerusalem is a powerful image of what can be achieved when we commit to dismantling oppression and building systems that honor the dignity and worth of all people, regardless of gender.

Revelation also challenges patriarchal readings of scripture that have historically justified women's subjugation. Its revolutionary themes of justice and equality call for a reimagining of religious narratives in ways that uplift and empower. By reclaiming Revelation as a text of resistance, we confront not only the societal structures that perpetuate gender inequality but also the theological frameworks that have supported them.

Applying Revelation to contemporary struggles for gender equality reframes it as a source of hope and action. Its critique of oppressive systems, its call to perseverance, and its vision of a just and inclusive world resonate powerfully in the ongoing fight for justice. Revelation reminds us that the work of dismantling patriarchy is sacred and that a world of equity and compassion is not only possible but divinely envisioned.

Revelation's Empowering Message

The book of Revelation, often misinterpreted as a harbinger of fear and finality, is fundamentally a text of hope, resilience, and empowerment. Its dramatic imagery and apocalyptic visions were written not to terrify, but to embolden oppressed communities, offering them the strength to resist and the promise of a better future. Revelation speaks to the enduring power of faith in the face of injustice, the transformative potential of collective action, and the certainty that oppressive systems, no matter how invincible they seem, will ultimately fall. For modern readers, its message is an inspiring call to embrace resilience and hope as tools for change and to unite in the shared work of building a world rooted in justice and compassion.

Revelation's enduring power lies in its vision of a just and inclusive future. The arrival of New Jerusalem (Revelation 21:1–4) represents the culmination of the struggle for liberation, a world where suffering and oppression are no more. This vision of a renewed creation is not a distant or unattainable dream but a tangible reminder that justice is possible. The imagery of open gates and a city that welcomes all speaks to the radical inclusivity of God's kingdom, challenging the hierarchies and exclusions that plague human systems. It reminds us that the work of justice is sacred and that collective efforts to dismantle oppression and build equity are aligned with divine purpose.

The hope offered by Revelation is not passive; it is active and deeply rooted in resilience. The text repeatedly emphasizes the need for perseverance in the face of adversity. The letters to the seven churches (Revelation 2–3) encourage communities to remain steadfast, promising that those who endure will share in the victory of justice. This call to resilience is as relevant today as it was for the early Christians who faced persecution under the Roman Empire. For those fighting against systemic injustices, whether rooted in gender inequality, racism, or economic exploitation, Revelation's message affirms the strength found in persistence and the power of refusing to accept oppression as inevitable.

Central to Revelation's empowering message is the theme of collective action. The text addresses communities, not individuals, underscoring the importance of solidarity in the struggle for justice. The vision of the multitude "from every nation, tribe, people and language" gathered before the throne (Revelation 7:9) celebrates the diversity and unity of those committed to liberation. This imagery serves as a reminder that transformative change is born from collective efforts, from the coming together of diverse voices to challenge injustice and build a new reality. Revelation calls us to recognize the strength of community, to amplify the voices of the marginalized, and to work together toward a shared vision of equity and inclusion.

Revelation's ultimate promise, that love and justice will triumph over oppression and corruption, offers profound hope for those engaged in the work of transformation. It reminds us that the systems we challenge, no matter how entrenched, are not eternal. Revelation's message is clear: the forces of empire and exploitation will fall, and a new world rooted in dignity, compassion, and equity will rise. This vision is not an abstraction; it is a call to action, inviting us to participate in its realization.

As we conclude this journey through Revelation, we are left with a powerful reminder of the sacredness of hope and the strength found in resilience and collective action. The text calls us to see beyond the chaos of the present, to imagine a better future, and to work tirelessly to bring it into being. Revelation empowers us to be co-creators of a world where justice flows like a river, where all are valued, and where love reigns supreme. It is a challenge, a promise, and a source of profound encouragement for all who seek to transform the world.

Conclusion to Reclaiming Power and Spirit
Synthesis

The journey through *Reclaiming Power and Spirit* illuminates a resounding truth: scripture, when reclaimed from patriarchal distortions, is a profound source of resistance, empowerment, and liberation. Throughout history, sacred texts have been used to oppress and silence, but they also hold the seeds of transformation for those willing to engage critically and courageously. This section has explored how scripture can empower women, inspire resistance against systemic injustice, and build a vision of collective liberation. Together, these themes form a powerful call to reclaim the sacred as a tool for dismantling oppression and creating a world rooted in justice, equity, and compassion.

Resistance is woven into the fabric of scripture, offering countless examples of individuals and communities who stood against unjust systems. From the psalms of protest that cry out for divine justice to the Exodus story's radical challenge to imperial domination, these texts invite us to resist the forces that dehumanize and exploit. Jesus' life and teachings further exemplify this resistance, as he confronted societal norms that marginalized women, the poor, and the oppressed. Reclaiming scripture is itself an act of resistance, an assertion that the sacred belongs to all and that its true power lies in its ability to challenge the status quo and inspire change. For modern readers, this resistance is both spiritual and practical, calling us to confront the systems of patriarchy, racism, and economic inequality that persist in our world.

Empowerment is another thread that runs through scripture, especially when reimagined through a lens of liberation. The stories of women like Miriam, Mary Magdalene, and the persistent widow demonstrate that faith is not passive but active, rooted in courage and agency. These women were not mere bystanders; they were leaders, witnesses, and agents of transformation. Their stories remind us that reclaiming scripture means reclaiming the voices and contributions of those who have been silenced or erased. Empowerment through scripture is not about conforming to traditional roles but about discovering the strength to challenge them and to envision new possibilities for oneself and one's community. It is about seeing oneself as part of a sacred story that affirms dignity, agency, and the right to flourish.

Liberation, the ultimate promise of scripture, ties these themes together. The texts explored in this section reveal a consistent vision of a world where justice prevails, where the marginalized are uplifted, and where systems of oppression are dismantled. Whether in the triumph of the Exodus, the parables of radical love and inclusion, or the apocalyptic vision of New Jerusalem, scripture consistently points toward liberation as both a divine mandate and a human responsibility. This vision is not an abstract ideal but a call to action, urging readers to participate in the ongoing work of justice and transformation. Liberation theology invites us to engage with scripture as a living, dynamic force that speaks to the realities of our time and equips us to confront them with faith and resolve.

The themes of resistance, empowerment, and liberation converge in a single powerful truth: the sacred is not a tool of control but a source of freedom. By reclaiming scripture, we reclaim our right to interpret it in ways that inspire justice, equality, and compassion. We assert that faith is not about submission to oppressive systems but about challenging them and creating alternatives that reflect the inclusive love of the divine.

As we conclude this exploration of *Reclaiming Power and Spirit*, we are left with both a challenge and a promise. The challenge is to continue this work, to resist oppression, to empower ourselves and others, and to commit to the collective task of liberation. The promise is that this work, rooted in the sacred, has the power to transform lives, communities, and the world. Scripture, reclaimed, is not a relic of the past but a blueprint for a future where justice and love reign supreme.

Call to Action

Scripture is not a relic of the past, locked in rigid interpretations and confined by patriarchal systems. It is a living text, vibrant and dynamic, with the power to inspire revolutionary change and challenge the forces of oppression. The sacred stories within it resonate across time, speaking to the struggles and aspirations of each generation. This call to action invites you to embrace scripture as a tool for justice and liberation, reclaiming its transformative power to confront patriarchy and build a more equitable and compassionate world.

For too long, scripture has been used to uphold systems of oppression, its messages distorted to justify the subjugation of women and marginalized groups. But the sacred texts themselves tell a different story, a story of resistance, empowerment, and the relentless pursuit of justice. Figures like Miriam, Mary Magdalene, the Samaritan woman at the well, and the persistent widow show us that faith is not about passive acceptance but about courage, agency, and the refusal to bow to injustice. These stories challenge patriarchal interpretations and invite us to see scripture as a source of strength and possibility.

Reclaiming scripture begins with the commitment to read it critically and courageously. Approach it not as a static set of rules but as a living conversation, rich with complexity and nuance. Ask the difficult questions: Whose voices have been amplified, and whose have been silenced? How have interpretations been shaped by power and privilege? How can these texts be reclaimed to speak to the realities of today's struggles? By engaging scripture in this way, you participate in a long tradition of readers who have wrestled with its meanings and found in it the seeds of liberation.

This work is not just about reclaiming scripture for ourselves; it is about sharing its transformative potential with others. Use these texts to challenge patriarchal norms and inspire revolutionary change in your communities. Share the stories of women in scripture as examples of faith and leadership. Highlight the themes of justice, equality, and inclusion that run through the sacred narratives. Encourage others to see scripture not as a tool of control but as a source of empowerment and hope. In doing so, you help to create a new theological and social framework that uplifts rather than oppresses.

Embracing scripture as a living text also calls us to action. Faith, as demonstrated in these sacred stories, is not passive; it is active, rooted in the pursuit of justice and the creation of a more equitable world. Let the parables of Jesus inspire you to confront systems of inequality and exclusion. Let the Psalms of lament and hope give voice to your struggles and aspirations. Let the vision of New Jerusalem in Revelation remind you of the possibility of a world where justice and love reign supreme. Scripture calls us to imagine such a world and to work tirelessly to bring it into being.

This call to action is both personal and collective. It invites you to reclaim your voice and your agency, to see yourself as part of the sacred story of resistance and liberation. It also challenges you to join with others in the work of dismantling patriarchy and building communities rooted in equity, compassion, and justice. The living text of scripture is not static or exclusive; it is expansive and inclusive, calling all of us to participate in its transformative power.

In reclaiming scripture, we reclaim the right to define our faith and use it as a force for good in the world. This is not just an act of resistance; it is an act of hope, a declaration that the sacred belongs to everyone and that its true purpose is to inspire love, justice, and revolutionary change. The challenge is clear, and the promise is profound: scripture, reclaimed, is a tool for liberation, and its power is yours to wield.

# Part III
*Drag the Patriarchy – Applying the FTP Lens*

Introduction to Dragging the Patriarchy
Overview of the FTP Lens

"Dragging the Patriarchy" is not merely a catchy phrase, it is a revolutionary framework for dismantling the oppressive systems that have defined and constrained our lives for centuries. Rooted in the *F**ck the Patriarchy (FTP) lens, this concept marries feminist theology with political resistance, creating a dynamic approach to confronting gender-based oppression and its intersection with other systems of domination. At its core, "Drag the Patriarchy" is a call to action, an invitation to expose the constructed nature of patriarchal power and to replace it with systems rooted in equity, justice, and liberation.

The FTP lens begins with the recognition that patriarchy is not an inevitable or natural order but a carefully constructed and maintained system designed to prioritize the power of a few over the dignity and agency of many. It infiltrates every facet of society, our laws, economies, religions, and cultural narratives, convincing us that its hierarchies are not only legitimate but divinely ordained. By dragging the patriarchy, we expose these falsehoods for what they are: tools of control, not reflections of truth. This process of unveiling the mechanisms of oppression is a radical act of resistance and a necessary step toward dismantling them.

At the intersection of feminist theology and political resistance, the FTP lens uses sacred texts and traditions as both a critique of patriarchal systems and a source of empowerment. For centuries, religion has been weaponized to maintain male dominance, with scripture selectively interpreted to silence women and justify their subjugation. Yet these same texts hold profound messages of liberation and justice when reclaimed and reimagined. Figures like Eve, Mary Magdalene, and the Samaritan woman at the well, often distorted into cautionary tales or symbols of submission, become icons of agency, resistance, and transformation when viewed through the FTP lens. Dragging the patriarchy means reclaiming these stories, unearthing their liberatory potential, and using them to challenge the systems that perpetuate inequality.

Politically, dragging the patriarchy demands direct confrontation with the structures that sustain gender oppression. From wage gaps and reproductive rights to representation in leadership and systemic violence, the tentacles of patriarchy reach far and wide. The FTP lens encourages bold, unapologetic resistance to these injustices, combining spiritual empowerment with practical activism. This is not a theoretical exercise; it is a call to disrupt the status quo, to protest, to organize, to educate, and to advocate for policies that create a more just and equitable world.

The concept of drag itself adds a layer of complexity and creativity to this work. Just as drag performance exposes the constructed nature of gender norms through exaggeration and subversion, dragging the patriarchy highlights the absurdity and fragility of its power. It reveals that patriarchy's dominance is not inherent or inevitable but a performance, a façade upheld by societal complicity. By dragging the patriarchy, we destabilize its foundations, forcing it to confront its own contradictions and collapse under the weight of its falsehoods.

"Drag the Patriarchy" is both a critique and a celebration. It critiques the systems that have silenced and oppressed, but it also celebrates the creativity, resilience, and courage of those who resist. It honors the long tradition of feminist theologians, activists, and visionaries who have paved the way for this work while calling all of us to join the struggle. The FTP lens is a reminder that dismantling patriarchy is not just about destruction, it is about building something better: a world where justice, compassion, and equality are not exceptions but norms.

As we embark on this exploration of dragging the patriarchy, let us carry the dual purpose of resistance and creation. Let us expose the systems that harm while envisioning and enacting the systems that heal. Dragging the patriarchy is not just a critique of power, it is a declaration of possibility, a call to reclaim the sacred and transform the world.

Scripture as a Tool for Liberation

Scripture, long used as a tool of oppression, holds immense potential to be reclaimed as a powerful instrument for liberation, activism, and personal growth. While its misinterpretation has justified patriarchal hierarchies and systemic injustice, its core messages of justice, equity, and compassion offer a blueprint for dismantling oppression and envisioning a better world. Reclaiming scripture as a tool for liberation means engaging with it critically, uncovering its transformative possibilities, and using its principles to inspire activism and foster personal growth. This process is not just about reinterpretation but about activating scripture as a living text that speaks directly to today's struggles.

Throughout history, scripture has been both a source of comfort for the oppressed and a rallying cry for justice. The story of the Exodus, for example, has inspired liberation movements around the world, from the abolition of slavery to the civil rights movement. Jesus' teachings on love, inclusion, and equality have been the foundation for feminist theology, LGBTQ+ advocacy, and efforts to confront economic inequality. These texts, when read through a lens of resistance and liberation, are not static relics but dynamic calls to action, urging us to confront the systems of power that perpetuate injustice.

For activism, scripture provides both a moral foundation and a language of resistance. Biblical principles such as justice for the poor, care for the marginalized, and opposition to tyranny resonate deeply with the goals of social movements. The prophetic tradition, from Isaiah to Amos, critiques systems of exploitation and calls for equitable distribution of resources. These texts remind us that faith is inherently political, not in the sense of partisan allegiance, but in its insistence on addressing systemic injustice. They challenge us to see activism as a sacred calling, an embodiment of the divine mandate to "let justice roll on like a river, righteousness like a never-failing stream" (Amos 5:24).

Practical applications of scripture in activism might include using its stories and principles to frame messages of justice, inspire collective action, or provide spiritual sustenance to those on the frontlines. The Psalms, for instance, offer prayers of lament and hope that can be adapted into modern protests and vigils. Parables like the Good Samaritan challenge societal indifference, urging us to care for the vulnerable. The vision of New Jerusalem in Revelation serves as a powerful metaphor for the inclusive and equitable world that activists strive to build. By reclaiming these texts, we infuse activism with a sense of purpose and connection to a larger, sacred narrative.

On a personal level, scripture serves as a tool for growth by challenging internalized narratives of unworthiness and oppression. Many women and marginalized individuals have been taught to see themselves as less than, unworthy of leadership, autonomy, or spiritual authority. Reclaiming scripture disrupts these narratives, offering stories of empowerment, such as Deborah's leadership, Mary Magdalene's role as the first witness to the resurrection, or the persistent widow's fight for justice. These stories affirm that faith is not about submission but about courage, agency, and the pursuit of justice.

Engaging scripture for personal growth also means using it as a source of resilience. Texts like the Psalms remind us that faith is not about suppressing pain or doubt but about bringing these emotions into dialogue with the divine. They teach us to lament injustice while holding onto hope, to persevere in the face of adversity, and to find strength in community and solidarity. This inner transformation fuels the outer work of activism, creating a holistic approach to liberation that integrates personal and collective growth.

By reclaiming scripture as a tool for liberation, we transform it from a weapon of oppression into an instrument of justice and healing. It becomes a guide for activism, a source of personal empowerment, and a reminder that the sacred is not static but alive, calling us to act, to grow, and to build a world where justice and compassion prevail.

Building Women's Liberation Theology
The Foundation

Liberation theology, at its heart, is a theological movement that emerges from the lived experiences of marginalized and oppressed communities, centering their struggles as the locus of divine action and revelation. Rooted in the belief that faith is inherently tied to justice, liberation theology challenges traditional theological frameworks that have often aligned with systems of power and privilege. Instead, it offers a vision of faith that confronts systemic oppression, uplifts the marginalized, and seeks to create a more equitable and compassionate world. When extended into feminist theology, liberation theology becomes a powerful tool for dismantling patriarchy, reclaiming women's voices, and building a framework for justice that addresses the intersectional realities of gender, race, class, and other forms of oppression.

The foundation of liberation theology lies in its origins within the struggles for social justice in Latin America during the mid-20th century. In the face of widespread poverty, political repression, and systemic inequality, theologians like Gustavo Gutiérrez articulated a vision of faith that was inseparable from the fight for justice. Gutiérrez's seminal work, *A Theology of Liberation*, emphasized the concept of a "preferential option for the poor," framing God as being uniquely present with those who are oppressed. Liberation theology insists that theology must be praxis-oriented, grounded in action and reflection, and that the Gospel is not just a spiritual message but a call to confront the structures of injustice that harm humanity.

Feminist theology, as an extension of liberation theology, builds on this foundation by centering the experiences and struggles of women, particularly in the face of patriarchal systems that have historically used religion to silence, oppress, and exclude them. Pioneers of feminist theology like Rosemary Radford Ruether and Elisabeth Schüssler Fiorenza challenged androcentric interpretations of scripture and tradition, arguing that theology must be reimagined to include women's voices and experiences. They critiqued the ways in which traditional theology has reinforced patriarchal structures, offering instead a vision of faith that uplifts women as full participants in the sacred and the social.

The historical struggles for gender justice provide the grounding for feminist liberation theology. From the suffrage movements to the fight for reproductive rights, women have long resisted systems that sought to control their bodies, silence their voices, and confine their roles. In the religious realm, this resistance has taken the form of reclaiming sacred texts, challenging exclusionary practices, and demanding equal participation in spiritual leadership. Feminist liberation theology emerges from these struggles, affirming that women's experiences are not peripheral but central to understanding the divine. It asserts that God is not a patriarchal figure upholding hierarchical systems but a liberator who seeks justice, equity, and the flourishing of all people.

One of the key contributions of feminist liberation theology is its focus on intersectionality, the recognition that gender oppression does not exist in isolation but intersects with race, class, sexuality, and other systems of power. This framework expands the scope of liberation theology, addressing the unique challenges faced by women of color, LGBTQ+ individuals, and other marginalized groups. It calls for a theology that is not only feminist but also anti-racist, anti-classist, and inclusive, reflecting the full diversity of human experience.

By grounding itself in historical struggles for justice, feminist liberation theology draws strength and inspiration from the resilience and creativity of women throughout history. Figures like Sojourner Truth, who combined spiritual conviction with political activism, embody the principles of feminist liberation theology in action. These women remind us that theology is not an abstract exercise but a lived practice, deeply connected to the realities of oppression and the work of liberation.

The foundation of feminist liberation theology is built on the belief that faith is a force for justice, not submission, for empowerment, not exclusion. It invites us to reimagine God, scripture, and community in ways that affirm the dignity and agency of all people, particularly those who have been marginalized. It challenges us to see theology as a tool for transformation, a means of resisting oppression and building a world where justice and equity prevail. This foundation is not static but dynamic, calling us to engage deeply with the past while acting boldly in the present to create a future of liberation and hope.

Women's Voices in Theology

Feminist thinkers have profoundly reshaped the field of theology by reinterpreting scripture to uncover and elevate themes of empowerment and resistance. These scholars and activists challenge patriarchal interpretations of sacred texts, demonstrating that scripture, when read through a feminist lens, contains profound messages of liberation, agency, and justice for women. Their work has reclaimed the voices and experiences of women in biblical narratives, transforming them from passive figures into powerful agents of change and resilience.

A central focus of feminist theology is reclaiming the narratives of women in scripture who have been misrepresented or marginalized by traditional interpretations. For example, the story of Eve in Genesis, long framed as the archetypal sinner responsible for humanity's fall, has been reexamined by feminist thinkers like Phyllis Trible. Trible highlights Eve's role as a seeker of knowledge and agency, arguing that her actions represent a courageous pursuit of understanding rather than disobedience. This reinterpretation challenges patriarchal narratives that have used Eve to justify the subjugation of women, instead presenting her as a figure of strength and complexity.

Similarly, Mary Magdalene has been reclaimed by feminist theologians as a leader and witness to the resurrection, rather than the repentant sinner she was long portrayed to be. Elisabeth Schüssler Fiorenza, a pioneer in feminist biblical scholarship, has emphasized Mary Magdalene's role as the "apostle to the apostles," highlighting her importance in the early Christian community. By restoring Mary Magdalene's leadership and spiritual authority, feminist thinkers challenge the erasure of women's contributions to religious history and affirm their rightful place as active participants in faith and ministry.

Feminist theology also draws attention to women in scripture who defied societal norms and acted with courage and resilience. The midwives Shiphrah and Puah in Exodus, who defied Pharaoh's order to kill Hebrew infants, are celebrated as examples of civil disobedience and moral conviction. Their story is a powerful reminder of the ways in which women have resisted oppressive systems throughout history, often at great personal risk. Similarly, the persistent widow in Luke 18, who demands justice from an indifferent judge, is reimagined as a symbol of resilience and advocacy, embodying the power of persistence in the face of systemic injustice.

Feminist thinkers have also reinterpreted scripture to uncover themes of mutuality and inclusivity that challenge hierarchical structures. Passages like Galatians 3:28, "There is neither Jew nor Gentile, neither slave nor free, nor is there male and female, for you are all one in Christ Jesus," are central to feminist theology's vision of equality. These texts provide a foundation for reimagining communities of faith where gender, race, and class do not determine one's worth or place in the divine order.

Beyond individual stories, feminist theologians critique the structural and cultural forces that have shaped scriptural interpretations. They emphasize that scripture is not inherently patriarchal but has been read and applied through the lens of male-dominated traditions. By engaging with the historical and cultural contexts of the Bible, feminist thinkers expose the ways in which patriarchal systems have distorted its messages and highlight its liberatory potential.

The work of feminist theologians is not confined to academic study; it has practical implications for how scripture is taught, preached, and lived. By reclaiming themes of empowerment and resistance, feminist theology equips individuals and communities to challenge oppressive systems and build spaces of inclusion and justice. It affirms that scripture belongs to everyone and that its transformative power is most fully realized when it uplifts the voices and experiences of those who have been silenced.

Through their reinterpretations, feminist thinkers inspire us to see scripture not as a tool of oppression but as a resource for liberation. Their work invites us to engage deeply with these sacred texts, to question traditional interpretations, and to find in them the strength to resist injustice and imagine new possibilities for faith and community.

Developing a Framework

A women's liberation theology that merges spiritual empowerment with political action is rooted in the belief that faith is inherently tied to the pursuit of justice and equity. It acknowledges that spiritual growth and political engagement are not separate spheres but interconnected aspects of a holistic approach to liberation.

*Centering Marginalized Voices*
At the heart of women's liberation theology is the commitment to center the voices, experiences, and struggles of marginalized women. This principle challenges the historical erasure and silencing of women within religious and societal narratives, emphasizing that their lived realities are vital to understanding both oppression and liberation. Women's experiences become the lens through which scripture is interpreted and theology is developed, ensuring that faith addresses real-world injustices.

*Reclaiming Sacred Texts*
A foundational principle of this theology is the reclamation of scripture as a source of empowerment rather than oppression. Patriarchal interpretations of sacred texts have often justified the subjugation of women, but a women's liberation theology reexamines these texts to uncover their liberatory potential. Figures like Mary Magdalene, Deborah, and the persistent widow are celebrated as leaders and agents of change, while themes of justice, mutuality, and inclusion are highlighted. Reclaiming these texts equips women with spiritual tools to resist injustice and advocate for equity.

*Intersectionality in Justice*
Women's liberation theology recognizes that gender oppression does not exist in isolation but intersects with race, class, sexuality, and other systems of power. Inspired by feminist and liberationist traditions, it adopts an intersectional approach, addressing the unique challenges faced by women of color, LGBTQ+ individuals, and those living in poverty. This principle ensures that the framework is inclusive and responsive to the diverse realities of oppression, advocating for justice in all its forms.

*Spiritual Empowerment*

This theology affirms that spiritual empowerment is integral to political resistance. Women are encouraged to reclaim their spiritual authority, recognizing themselves as co-creators in the divine mission of justice and liberation. Prayer, reflection, and ritual are not passive acts but sources of strength, resilience, and inspiration for action. Spiritual empowerment also involves redefining theological concepts, such as God, sin, and salvation, in ways that affirm women's dignity and agency.

*Faith as Praxis*

A women's liberation theology insists that faith must be lived out through action. It draws on the liberation theology principle of praxis, a cycle of reflection and action, to address systemic injustice. This involves engaging in political advocacy, community organizing, and direct action to challenge patriarchy, racism, economic exploitation, and other forms of oppression. Faith is not confined to the personal or spiritual realm; it is a call to transform society.

*Community and Solidarity*

The framework emphasizes the importance of building communities of mutual support and solidarity. Liberation is not an individual endeavor but a collective process that requires collaboration across identities and movements. Faith communities become spaces where individuals can share their struggles, celebrate their victories, and find strength in collective action. This principle affirms the power of unity in the pursuit of justice.

*Vision of Liberation*

Finally, women's liberation theology is grounded in a vision of liberation that is both spiritual and material. It seeks to dismantle oppressive systems while building equitable alternatives that reflect the values of justice, love, and inclusion. This vision is inspired by scripture, such as the vision of New Jerusalem in Revelation, and calls for the creation of a world where all people are free to flourish.

By merging spiritual empowerment with political action, women's liberation theology becomes a dynamic force for transformation. It calls individuals and communities to challenge oppression, reclaim their faith, and work together to create a more just and compassionate world.

120

Scripture as a Call to Resistance

Scripture, when read through the lens of liberation theology, emerges as a profound call to resistance against patriarchal structures and other systems of oppression. Far from being a text that mandates submission to unjust hierarchies, the Bible contains narratives that confront power, uplift the marginalized, and envision a world rooted in justice. These stories offer a powerful critique of patriarchy and inspire action to dismantle systems of inequality. By examining key biblical narratives, we see how scripture challenges oppression and calls individuals and communities to engage in transformative resistance.

One of the most striking examples is the story of the Hebrew midwives, Shiphrah and Puah, in the book of Exodus (Exodus 1:15–21). Ordered by Pharaoh to kill all male Hebrew infants, these women defied the most powerful ruler of their time. Their act of civil disobedience, rooted in their reverence for God, saved countless lives and set the stage for the liberation of the Israelites. Shiphrah and Puah's story highlights the moral courage required to confront oppressive systems, demonstrating that resistance to injustice is a sacred act. These women, often overlooked in patriarchal readings of scripture, embody the principle that faith is not about compliance but about challenging structures of domination.

The narrative of Queen Esther provides another example of scripture as a call to resistance (Esther 4:1–17). Esther, a young Jewish woman, risks her life to confront King Xerxes and expose Haman's plot to annihilate her people. Her journey from reluctant participant to bold advocate underscores the importance of agency and courage in the face of systemic oppression. Encouraged by her cousin Mordecai to recognize her role in the broader struggle for justice, "Who knows but that you have come to your royal position for such a time as this?" Esther exemplifies how individuals can leverage their positions of influence to challenge patriarchal and genocidal structures. Her story inspires modern readers to act boldly in the pursuit of justice, even when the stakes are high.

The Gospels are replete with examples of Jesus directly confronting patriarchy and elevating marginalized voices, especially women's. In Luke 7:36–50, Jesus defends a woman labeled as a sinner who anoints him with perfume in a Pharisee's house. While others judge and dismiss her, Jesus affirms her actions as a profound expression of love and faith. His words, "Your faith has saved you; go in peace," overturn societal norms that sought to devalue and shame her. This narrative challenges the patriarchal practice of defining women solely by their reputations or perceived morality, offering instead a vision of inclusion, forgiveness, and empowerment.

The story of the persistent widow in Luke 18:1–8 provides a direct metaphor for resistance. In this parable, a widow—a symbol of vulnerability in the ancient world—demands justice from a corrupt judge who neither fears God nor respects people. Through her persistence, she ultimately secures what is rightfully hers. Jesus uses this parable to illustrate the power of tenacity in the face of systemic injustice, affirming that even the most marginalized individuals can enact change through steadfast action. For those confronting patriarchal structures today, this story is a reminder that resistance requires perseverance and unwavering commitment.

Finally, Revelation's vision of New Jerusalem (Revelation 21:1–4) encapsulates the ultimate call to resistance against all forms of systemic oppression, including patriarchy. This vision of a renewed world, where "there will be no more death or mourning or crying or pain," serves as a blueprint for liberation. It calls believers to actively resist the "Babylons" of their time, empires and systems built on exploitation and inequality, and to work toward a world where justice and love prevail.

These biblical narratives demonstrate that scripture is not static or complicit with oppression; it is dynamic and transformative, calling individuals and communities to resist patriarchal structures and pursue justice. Liberation theology embraces these stories as evidence that faith is a force for change, urging us to confront injustice with courage, resilience, and hope.

Application in Communities

Women's liberation theology offers a powerful framework for inspiring activism, building communities, and fostering interfaith solidarity. Grounded in the pursuit of justice, equity, and inclusion, it equips women and their allies to address systemic oppression while cultivating spaces of empowerment and mutual support.

In activism, women's liberation theology provides both spiritual grounding and practical tools. By reclaiming scriptural narratives of resistance and empowerment, it challenges patriarchal norms and inspires action against injustices like gender-based violence, wage inequality, and political exclusion. Activists can draw on the stories of biblical figures like Esther, Mary Magdalene, and the persistent widow as examples of courage and perseverance in the face of systemic oppression. This theology also fosters resilience, reminding activists that their work is not only practical but sacred, aligning with a divine call for justice.

Community building is central to women's liberation theology. By creating spaces that prioritize inclusion and mutual support, this framework helps women and marginalized individuals share their stories, organize around common goals, and celebrate their unique strengths. Faith communities that embrace women's liberation theology become places where individuals feel valued and empowered to challenge systemic inequalities together. These communities provide a foundation for nurturing leadership, promoting education, and amplifying voices often silenced in traditional settings.

Interfaith solidarity is another critical aspect. Women's liberation theology recognizes that the fight for justice transcends religious boundaries, inviting collaboration across diverse traditions. It emphasizes shared values of compassion, dignity, and equity, creating opportunities for dialogue and joint action. By uniting around common goals, interfaith communities can address systemic issues like poverty, discrimination, and violence, amplifying their impact through collective strength.

Ultimately, women's liberation theology transforms faith into a catalyst for action, empowering individuals and communities to create a more just and equitable world.

Practical Steps

Initiating discussions and workshops rooted in women's liberation theology requires intentionality, inclusivity, and a clear focus on empowerment and action.

Define the Purpose and Goals
Begin by clarifying the purpose of your discussion or workshop. Are you reclaiming scriptural narratives, addressing gender inequality, or fostering interfaith collaboration? Define specific goals, such as empowering participants to recognize their agency.

Create a Welcoming Space
Ensure the environment is inclusive and safe, where participants feel valued and heard. Use gender-neutral language, provide accommodations for accessibility, and establish ground rules for respectful dialogue. Recognize the diversity of experiences within the group and honor intersectional perspectives.

Start with Scripture
Introduce a key biblical narrative that resonates with themes of liberation, such as the stories of Shiphrah and Puah, Esther, or the persistent widow. Read the text collectively, then encourage participants to share their interpretations, focusing on empowerment and resistance.

Encourage Personal Connections
Invite participants to reflect on how the text relates to their own experiences or struggles. Use prompts like, "What does this story teach us about confronting injustice in our own lives?"

Promote Actionable Steps
Guide the group in brainstorming ways to apply the discussion to their communities. This might include organizing advocacy campaigns, creating inclusive spaces in faith communities, or engaging in interfaith collaborations.

Build Ongoing Engagement
Encourage participants to stay connected, forming a network for mutual support and shared action. Schedule follow-up sessions to deepen the discussion and measure progress.

Rituals of Rebellion - Redefining Worship
Introduction to Rituals of Rebellion

Rituals of rebellion challenge the boundaries of traditional worship by reimagining practices to reflect feminist and inclusive values. Worship has long been a space shaped by patriarchal norms, often silencing women's voices, excluding marginalized communities, and reinforcing power structures that prioritize control over collective liberation. However, worship can also be a site of radical transformation, a sacred act of resistance where the marginalized reclaim their spiritual agency, redefine their relationship with the divine, and envision a more equitable world. By reimagining worship through the lens of feminist theology, rituals of rebellion create inclusive spaces where justice, equality, and empowerment take center stage.

Reimagining worship begins with recognizing that traditional practices often reflect and perpetuate exclusionary norms. Language, leadership roles, and rituals in many faith communities have historically prioritized male authority, often portraying God in exclusively patriarchal terms and limiting women's participation. These practices subtly reinforce the idea that spirituality is hierarchical and that access to the divine is mediated through rigid power structures. Feminist theology challenges this paradigm by insisting that worship must reflect the full diversity of human experience and that all voices, especially those historically silenced, deserve a place in the sacred narrative.

At the heart of rituals of rebellion is the intentional use of inclusive language and imagery to represent the divine. This involves moving beyond patriarchal descriptions of God as male and embracing metaphors and names that affirm God's presence in all genders, races, and identities. Describing God as Creator, Sustainer, Wisdom, or even as a nurturing mother expands the spiritual imagination and challenges the limitations of patriarchal theology. Inclusive language in prayers, hymns, and liturgies ensures that everyone in the community feels seen and valued, fostering a deeper connection to the divine and one another.

Leadership in worship is another critical area for redefinition. Rituals of rebellion affirm that spiritual authority is not tied to gender or hierarchy but to the gifts and callings of all individuals. Women,

LGBTQ+ individuals, and others excluded from traditional leadership roles are empowered to lead prayers, preach, and shape communal worship experiences. This redistribution of authority not only challenges patriarchal norms but also enriches worship by bringing diverse perspectives and experiences into sacred spaces. When leadership reflects the community's diversity, worship becomes a celebration of inclusion and shared spiritual power.

The content and structure of worship are also vital to reimagining rituals. Traditional liturgies often focus on themes of submission, guilt, and individual salvation, which can reinforce harmful narratives for women and marginalized groups. Rituals of rebellion, by contrast, center on themes of empowerment, justice, and collective liberation. Prayers of lament give voice to the pain of oppression, while prayers of hope and resistance inspire courage and action. Communal acts, such as sharing personal testimonies, lighting candles for justice, or incorporating art and music from diverse cultures, create a worship experience that honors both the struggles and strengths of the community.

Finally, rituals of rebellion integrate activism into worship. Faith and justice are deeply intertwined, and worship can become a launching point for collective action. Blessings for protestors, reflections on systemic inequality, and calls to action transform worship from a passive experience into an active commitment to change. By linking spiritual practices with social justice, rituals of rebellion affirm that worship is not only about connecting with the divine but also about embodying divine values in the world.

Redefining worship through rituals of rebellion is an act of liberation. It reclaims sacred spaces as places where all are welcome, all are valued, and all are empowered to act. These rituals challenge oppressive norms, celebrate diversity, and create a vision of worship that reflects feminist and inclusive values, turning faith into a dynamic force for justice and transformation.

Analyzing Traditional Rituals

Traditional worship practices, while central to many faith communities, often reflect and reinforce patriarchal norms that perpetuate exclusion, hierarchy, and control. These rituals, rooted in centuries-old structures, have frequently marginalized women and other oppressed groups, presenting worship as a space shaped by power dynamics rather than mutuality and inclusion. By critically analyzing these practices, we can uncover the ways they uphold patriarchal ideologies and explore pathways for creating worship that embodies equity and liberation.

One of the most glaring features of traditional worship is the consistent use of patriarchal language and imagery to describe the divine. God is often exclusively referred to as "Father," "King," or "Lord," perpetuating the notion that divinity is inherently male and authority is intrinsically tied to masculinity. These titles not only alienate those who do not see themselves reflected in such imagery but also reinforce the cultural association of power, leadership, and control with male identity. Feminist theology critiques this one-dimensional portrayal, arguing that it limits the spiritual imagination and diminishes the diverse ways people can experience and relate to the divine.

Leadership roles in traditional worship further entrench patriarchal norms. Many religious traditions restrict positions of spiritual authority, such as clergy, pastors, or elders, to men, relegating women to secondary roles or excluding them entirely. Even in communities where women are permitted to lead, they often face scrutiny, resistance, or tokenization. This perpetuates a harmful hierarchy that suggests spiritual insight and authority are tied to gender, reinforcing the subjugation of women within both religious and societal contexts. These practices not only silence women but also rob communities of the richness that diverse leadership brings to worship.

The structure and content of traditional rituals often emphasize themes of submission and guilt, which can have harmful implications for marginalized groups, particularly women. Prayers, hymns, and sermons frequently focus on obedience, repentance, and the relinquishing of individual agency. While these themes may hold spiritual significance, they have historically been used to justify women's submission to patriarchal authority—whether in the family, the church, or society at large. Women have been taught to see themselves as inherently flawed or sinful, reinforcing narratives of inadequacy and dependence that limit their agency and spiritual empowerment.

Traditional worship also tends to exclude the voices and experiences of marginalized groups. Liturgies, hymns, and prayers often reflect the perspectives of dominant cultural and social groups, leaving little room for diverse expressions of faith. Women's experiences, particularly those of women of color, LGBTQ+ individuals, or those from economically disadvantaged backgrounds, are rarely acknowledged or celebrated in traditional worship settings. This exclusion creates a disconnect between the sacred and the lived realities of many worshippers, diminishing the transformative potential of worship as a space of healing and liberation.

Finally, traditional rituals often separate worship from action, presenting faith as a private, spiritual matter disconnected from social justice. By focusing solely on personal salvation or individual morality, these practices neglect the communal and systemic dimensions of faith. This separation can perpetuate patriarchal systems by failing to challenge the structures of inequality and oppression that exist within and beyond the church. Worship that does not address these injustices risks becoming complicit in their perpetuation.

Critiquing traditional worship practices is not an attack on faith but an invitation to reimagine it. By identifying the patriarchal norms embedded in these rituals, we can begin to create worship that is inclusive, empowering, and transformative. This involves rethinking language, expanding leadership, centering diverse experiences, and connecting worship with justice. Worship has the potential to be a space of radical liberation, a place where all voices are heard, all experiences are valued, and all are empowered to act in the name of love and justice. Through this transformation, worship can truly reflect the divine vision of equity and inclusion.

Creating Inclusive Practices

Creating inclusive practices in worship involves reimagining rituals and ceremonies to reflect the values of feminism, diversity, and intersectionality. These practices celebrate the richness of human experiences and challenge traditional norms that have excluded or marginalized women, people of color, LGBTQ+ individuals, and other oppressed groups. By incorporating diverse voices, symbols, and narratives, inclusive rituals create sacred spaces that affirm dignity, foster connection, and inspire collective action.

*Inclusive Naming of the Divine*
Begin ceremonies with prayers and invocations that use diverse and inclusive names for God, reflecting a range of cultural, gendered, and non-gendered metaphors. Instead of relying solely on terms like "Father" or "Lord," incorporate names like Creator, Sustainer, Wisdom, Nurturer, or even culturally specific terms such as El Shaddai, Sophia, or Great Spirit. These names invite worshippers to imagine and connect with the divine in ways that transcend patriarchal limitations, affirming the sacred in all genders and identities.

*Rituals Honoring Women's Stories*
Design ceremonies that explicitly honor the contributions, struggles, and resilience of women, both in scripture and in contemporary life. For example, a "Women of the Word" service could center the stories of figures like Deborah, Mary Magdalene, Shiphrah, and Puah, pairing their narratives with reflections on modern women's activism and leadership. These rituals might include the lighting of candles for each woman's story, symbolic gestures of empowerment (like the laying on of hands), or communal affirmations celebrating women's agency and spiritual authority.

*Intersectional Storytelling and Testimonies*
Incorporate storytelling as a central element of worship, inviting participants to share their personal experiences, particularly those shaped by intersecting identities. Create space for voices that have historically been excluded, such as women of color, LGBTQ+ individuals, and people with disabilities. These testimonies can be woven into the liturgy, paired with scripture or sacred readings that resonate with themes of liberation and resilience. By centering diverse

perspectives, these rituals affirm the sacredness of all experiences and foster a sense of solidarity and shared purpose.

*Collaborative Art and Music*
Use art and music as tools to celebrate diversity and intersectionality in worship. Collaborative projects, such as creating a community mural or weaving a tapestry of ribbons symbolizing participants' identities and struggles, can visually represent the beauty of collective liberation. Music selections should draw from diverse traditions, incorporating hymns, chants, and songs from various cultures, languages, and genres. Inviting women composers, queer musicians, or artists from underrepresented communities to lead these elements ensures that worship reflects a breadth of human expression.

*Rituals of Healing and Solidarity*
Inclusive ceremonies can also address collective trauma and foster healing, particularly for those who have experienced oppression or exclusion. Consider holding a "Ritual of Release," where participants write down harmful messages they've internalized (e.g., about gender or identity) and symbolically release them, perhaps by burning or shredding the papers. Follow this with a "Ritual of Affirmation," where participants receive blessings, affirmations, or symbols of empowerment, such as anointing with oil or tying a string around the wrist to symbolize community support.

*Justice-Oriented Ceremonies*
Connect worship directly to activism by incorporating rituals that inspire and bless acts of justice. For example, before a protest or advocacy event, hold a "Blessing of the Activists" ceremony, where participants receive words of encouragement and strength for their work. Similarly, a "Liturgy of Solidarity" could focus on prayers and commitments to action on issues like reproductive justice, racial equity, or environmental sustainability.

*Seasonal Celebrations of Feminist Values*
Reimagine traditional holidays and sacred seasons to emphasize themes of inclusion and justice. For instance, create a feminist Advent celebration focusing on women's prophetic voices, or reinterpret Easter as a celebration of resilience and new beginnings, centering Mary Magdalene as the first witness to the resurrection.

Spiritual Empowerment through Ritual

Redefined worship practices centered on spiritual empowerment have the potential to transform both individuals and communities, fostering personal growth and collective action. By challenging traditional norms and creating inclusive, justice-oriented spaces, these practices invite participants to connect deeply with the divine, themselves, and one another, inspiring meaningful change.

For individuals, redefined rituals provide a foundation for personal empowerment. Inclusive language, diverse symbols, and narratives that affirm all identities help participants see themselves as sacred and valued. Practices like communal affirmations, meditative reflections, or rituals of release and affirmation allow individuals to confront internalized oppression, heal from past harms, and embrace their agency. When participants hear their own stories echoed in the liturgy or witness leadership by those who share their lived experiences, they are reminded that they are integral to the divine story of justice and liberation.

Collectively, these reimagined rituals cultivate a sense of shared purpose and solidarity. Worship becomes a space where communities celebrate diversity, engage in honest storytelling, and unite around common goals. Practices like collaborative art projects, storytelling circles, or justice-oriented blessings foster bonds of mutual support and inspire collective action. Rituals that tie spiritual practices to social justice, such as prayers for activists, vigils for marginalized communities, or symbolic actions like planting trees or lighting candles for justice, demonstrate how faith can drive transformative work in the world.

Ultimately, spiritual empowerment through ritual is about reclaiming worship as a dynamic, liberatory force. It bridges personal healing with communal strength, reminding participants that they are both deeply loved and profoundly capable of enacting change. These practices inspire resilience, courage, and hope, empowering individuals and communities to grow, resist injustice, and build a world rooted in equity and compassion.

Celebrating Women's Stories

Incorporating women's biblical narratives into worship is a powerful
way to celebrate their resilience, leadership, and vital role in the
sacred story of faith. These narratives, often overlooked or
misinterpreted in traditional worship, provide rich opportunities to
honor women's contributions and inspire communities with their
courage and agency. By centering these stories, worship becomes a
space of empowerment and inclusion, affirming the sacred value of
women's voices and experiences.

To celebrate women's stories, worship can focus on key biblical
figures whose lives embody resilience and leadership. For example, a
service could highlight Miriam's courage in guiding Moses to safety,
pairing her story with reflections on modern women leading
movements for justice. Another could focus on Deborah, the prophet
and judge, exploring how her leadership challenges gender norms and
inspires women's leadership in faith and society today. Mary
Magdalene's role as the first witness to the resurrection can be
honored during Easter, emphasizing her spiritual authority and
groundbreaking role in early Christianity.

Rituals can make these stories tangible and participatory. Lighting
candles for each woman's story, reading their narratives aloud in a
communal setting, or inviting participants to reflect on how these
women inspire their own lives can create meaningful engagement.
Music and art can further amplify these themes, incorporating hymns,
poetry, or visual representations inspired by these figures.

Celebrating women's stories not only reclaims their place in scripture
but also honors the women in our communities who embody similar
strength and leadership. These practices affirm that women's voices
are integral to faith and inspire all participants to embrace their own
resilience and agency in the ongoing story of justice and liberation.

Practical Guidance

Designing inclusive and empowering rituals requires intentional planning, a commitment to diversity, and a focus on active participation.

Ritual of Affirmation
Purpose: To affirm the dignity and worth of all participants.
Steps:
Begin with a reading or reflection that celebrates diversity and inclusion, such as Galatians 3:28 or a feminist poem.
Provide small tokens (stones, ribbons, or flowers) for participants to hold as symbols of their unique identities.
Create a circle and invite participants to affirm one another with simple statements, such as "You are seen," "You are valued," or "You are loved."
Close with a collective prayer or chant celebrating community and resilience.

Candle-Lighting for Justice
Purpose: To honor struggles and inspire action for justice.
Steps:
Arrange candles in a central space, each representing a cause or group (e.g., women's rights, racial justice, LGBTQ+ inclusion).
Invite participants to light a candle, offering a prayer, statement, or moment of silence for the cause.
Conclude with a collective commitment to specific actions supporting justice in the highlighted areas.

Storytelling Circle
Purpose: To celebrate women's stories and create space for diverse voices.
Steps:
Select a biblical narrative featuring women's resilience (e.g., Deborah, Ruth, or the persistent widow).
Pair the story with reflections from modern women in the community or historical figures.
Invite participants to share their own experiences of resilience and leadership.
Close with a group blessing acknowledging the strength in shared stories.

FTP in Action - Using Scripture to Challenge Power Structures The Power of Biblical Language

The power of biblical language lies in its ability to resonate deeply with individuals and communities, transcending time and culture. Rooted in rich traditions of justice, liberation, and moral clarity, scripture has often been invoked to inspire resistance and challenge oppressive power structures. When reclaimed through the lens of feminist theology and liberation ethics, biblical language becomes a potent tool for critiquing authoritarian policies and advocating for justice. It not only critiques systems of domination but also uplifts alternative visions of equity, compassion, and shared humanity.

Throughout history, biblical language has been a cornerstone of resistance movements. In the United States, abolitionists invoked the Exodus story to confront the dehumanizing institution of slavery, framing their struggle as a modern-day liberation from Pharaoh's grip. Civil rights leaders like Dr. Martin Luther King Jr. echoed prophetic calls for justice, drawing from Amos' demand to "let justice roll on like a river" (Amos 5:24) to expose the hypocrisy of a nation built on inequity. These examples illustrate how scripture's moral authority can be used to hold systems accountable and inspire collective action.

In contemporary struggles, biblical language continues to challenge authoritarian policies that perpetuate injustice. Consider the parable of the Good Samaritan (Luke 10:25–37), which dismantles exclusionary ideologies by elevating the marginalized as moral exemplars. This story critiques policies that neglect or exploit the vulnerable, urging us to ask, "Who is our neighbor?" in the context of immigration reform, healthcare access, or systemic poverty. By highlighting the moral duty to care for the "other," this parable undermines authoritarian narratives that dehumanize and divide.

The prophetic tradition of scripture is particularly powerful in critiquing systems of corruption and exploitation. Texts like Isaiah 10:1–2, "Woe to those who make unjust laws, to those who issue oppressive decrees,"speak directly to the policies that prioritize power and profit over human dignity. These verses provide a foundation for confronting laws and practices that harm the most vulnerable, such as discriminatory legislation, environmental degradation, or attacks on reproductive rights. By framing justice as a divine mandate, biblical language galvanizes resistance against policies that betray the sacred values of equity and care.

Scripture also offers an alternative vision of governance rooted in humility and service, directly opposing authoritarian ideals of dominance and control. Jesus' teaching that "whoever wants to become great among you must be your servant" (Matthew 20:26) redefines leadership as an act of service, challenging power structures that prioritize self-interest and oppression. This ethic of servant leadership provides a framework for advocating policies that uplift communities rather than exploit them, reminding us that true power lies in compassion and accountability.

The poetic and symbolic nature of biblical language enhances its rhetorical power, making it a compelling tool for activism. Metaphors like the "light of the world" (Matthew 5:14) or the "valley of dry bones" (Ezekiel 37:1–14) inspire hope and action, connecting spiritual renewal with systemic transformation. These images can be woven into speeches, protests, and community organizing efforts to evoke a shared sense of purpose and resilience. They remind us that the fight for justice is both practical and deeply spiritual, rooted in the belief that liberation is not only possible but divinely envisioned.

For women and marginalized groups, reclaiming biblical language is particularly empowering. It disrupts patriarchal and authoritarian interpretations that have been used to silence and control, replacing them with messages of empowerment, equality, and resistance. By wielding scripture to challenge power structures, women and their allies assert their rightful place in the sacred narrative and amplify their voices in the struggle for justice.

The power of biblical language lies in its ability to inspire, unite, and confront. Reclaimed and reimagined, it becomes a formidable tool for resisting authoritarian policies and advocating for a world where justice, equity, and compassion prevail. Its words do not merely echo in ancient times; they speak to the heart of today's struggles, urging us to act with courage and conviction.

Historical Examples

Biblical texts have been a cornerstone of movements for social change throughout history, providing moral authority, inspiration, and a unifying language for those fighting oppression and injustice. When wielded as tools of liberation, scripture's messages of justice, equality, and resistance have galvanized communities to challenge entrenched systems of power. From the abolitionist movement to civil rights struggles and modern advocacy for gender and racial equality, biblical texts have consistently empowered transformative movements.

The Abolitionist Movement
The story of the Exodus, in which Moses leads the Israelites out of Egyptian bondage, was a central biblical narrative for the abolitionist movement. Enslaved African Americans and abolitionist leaders alike invoked the cry, "Let my people go" (Exodus 9:1), as a rallying call against the dehumanizing institution of slavery. Spirituals like "Go Down, Moses" turned this text into an anthem of resistance, embedding the biblical promise of deliverance into the cultural fabric of the fight for freedom. Abolitionist preachers used texts like Isaiah 61:1, "The Spirit of the Sovereign Lord is on me, because the Lord has anointed me to proclaim good news to the poor. He has sent me to bind up the brokenhearted, to proclaim freedom for the captives," to frame the emancipation of enslaved people as a divine mandate.

The Civil Rights Movement
The civil rights movement of the mid-20th century heavily relied on biblical texts to challenge segregation and systemic racism. Dr. Martin Luther King Jr., a Baptist minister, frequently drew on scripture to articulate the moral imperative of racial justice. His "I Have a Dream" speech echoes the imagery of Amos 5:24: "Let justice roll on like a river, righteousness like a never-failing stream." This prophetic text condemned the hypocrisy of leaders who upheld discriminatory policies while professing faith. King also invoked Exodus, identifying Black Americans' struggle for civil rights with the Israelites' journey from slavery to freedom. His use of biblical language transformed scripture into a powerful tool for exposing injustice and inspiring collective action.

The Suffrage Movement
Biblical texts also played a role in the women's suffrage movement.
Leaders like Sojourner Truth, a former enslaved woman and
outspoken advocate for both abolition and women's rights, used
scripture to challenge patriarchal interpretations that excluded
women from public and political life. In her famous speech, "Ain't I a
Woman?" Truth asked, "Where did your Christ come from? From
God and a woman. Man had nothing to do with Him." Her
rhetorical use of Mary's role in the birth of Christ turned scripture
into a critique of male-dominated power structures and an affirmation
of women's agency and equality.

Liberation Theology in Latin America
In the 20th century, liberation theology emerged in Latin America,
using scripture to address systemic poverty and political oppression.
The Exodus story, the prophetic texts, and Jesus' teachings on the
poor became central to this movement. Gustavo Gutiérrez and other
theologians emphasized the "preferential option for the poor,"
framing the struggle for economic justice as a divine imperative. Luke
4:18, in which Jesus declares, "The Spirit of the Lord is on me,
because he has anointed me to proclaim good news to the poor," was
used to challenge exploitative regimes and inspire grassroots
organizing.

Modern Social Justice Movements
Biblical texts continue to inspire contemporary movements for gender
equality, LGBTQ+ rights, and environmental justice. The parable of
the Good Samaritan (Luke 10:25–37) is invoked in debates about
immigration and healthcare, challenging policies that neglect the
vulnerable. Texts like Galatians 3:28, "There is neither Jew nor
Gentile, neither slave nor free, nor is there male and female, for you
are all one in Christ Jesus," are used to advocate for inclusion and
equality, confronting patriarchal and exclusionary ideologies.

Strategies for Activism

Scripture can be a powerful tool in activism, lending moral authority and emotional resonance to public speeches, writings, and campaigns aimed at challenging systemic oppression. By reclaiming its liberatory themes and using them strategically, activists can inspire change and foster solidarity.

*Incorporate Prophetic Texts in Public Speeches*
Use prophetic texts like Amos 5:24—"Let justice roll on like a river"—to highlight the moral imperative of justice. Frame systemic issues such as racial inequality, gender discrimination, or environmental degradation as violations of divine principles. Pair these texts with contemporary examples of injustice to connect timeless wisdom with present-day struggles, making the call for action both urgent and grounded.

*Reimagine Parables in Writings*
Reinterpret parables like the Good Samaritan (Luke 10:25–37) to address modern issues such as immigration or healthcare. Write op-eds or essays that draw parallels between the Samaritan's compassion and today's responsibilities toward marginalized communities. Use these narratives to challenge policies that neglect the vulnerable, positioning compassion as a moral and spiritual duty.

*Create Campaign Slogans with Scriptural Roots*
Design campaign messaging that echoes scripture's calls for liberation. For example, a reproductive justice campaign could use Galatians 5:1, "It is for freedom that Christ has set us free," to frame autonomy and choice as divinely supported rights. Short, powerful phrases rooted in scripture resonate with audiences while grounding activism in moral principles.

*Use Scripture in Protests and Vigils*
Incorporate scripture into signs, chants, and prayers during protests and vigils. For example, display Exodus 3:7, "I have seen the misery of my people," to demand justice for oppressed groups. Scriptural language amplifies the moral urgency of activism while fostering spiritual solidarity.

Case Studies

Biblical rhetoric has been successfully used in activism to inspire movements, challenge systemic oppression, and galvanize communities for change. These case studies illustrate how scripture can provide moral authority and a shared language for justice.

*The Civil Rights Movement*
Dr. Martin Luther King Jr. masterfully employed biblical rhetoric to challenge segregation and racial injustice. In his *"I Have a Dream"* speech, he referenced Amos 5:24, "Let justice roll on like a river, righteousness like a never-failing stream," to frame racial equality as a divine mandate. By invoking scripture, King connected the fight for civil rights to a higher moral authority, uniting a diverse audience around the shared principle of justice. His use of Exodus imagery, paralleling the civil rights struggle to the Israelites' liberation from Egypt, further underscored the movement's moral urgency and divine alignment.

*Liberation Theology in Latin America*
During the 20th-century liberation theology movement, leaders like Archbishop Óscar Romero used scripture to confront poverty and political repression. Romero's sermons frequently referenced Luke 4:18, where Jesus declares, "He has sent me to proclaim freedom for the prisoners and recovery of sight for the blind, to set the oppressed free." This biblical rhetoric framed social justice as a divine mission, inspiring grassroots resistance against corrupt regimes and empowering impoverished communities to demand systemic change.

*Immigration Advocacy*
Modern immigration activists have drawn on Matthew 25:35, "I was a stranger, and you welcomed me," to challenge xenophobic policies and advocate for the humane treatment of migrants. This verse has appeared on protest signs, in speeches, and during vigils, connecting faith communities to the broader cause of immigration justice and framing hospitality as a sacred responsibility.

These examples demonstrate how biblical rhetoric, rooted in justice and liberation, can powerfully amplify activism and inspire collective action.

Engaging with Opponents

Countering patriarchal interpretations of scripture in debates and discussions requires a combination of preparation, empathy, and critical engagement. The goal is not only to challenge oppressive readings but also to illuminate scripture's liberatory themes and encourage deeper reflection. Here are effective strategies:

*Know the Texts and Contexts*
Familiarize yourself with commonly cited passages used to justify patriarchy, such as 1 Timothy 2:12 ("I do not permit a woman to teach") or Ephesians 5:22 ("Wives, submit yourselves to your own husbands"). Research their historical, cultural, and literary contexts to expose how these verses have been misinterpreted or applied selectively. For instance, explain how Paul's letters were shaped by specific community issues and are not blanket prescriptions for all time.

*Highlight Alternative Biblical Narratives*
Introduce stories of women in scripture who exercised agency and leadership, such as Deborah, a judge and prophet (Judges 4–5), or Mary Magdalene, the first witness to the resurrection (John 20:1–18). These examples challenge the notion that scripture inherently supports women's subordination and reveal the richness of women's roles in biblical history.

*Reclaim the Language of Liberation*
Frame scripture as a text that prioritizes justice and equality. Use passages like Galatians 3:28, "There is neither male nor female, for you are all one in Christ Jesus," to counter patriarchal claims and emphasize the inclusive nature of the Gospel.

*Appeal to Shared Values*
Focus on common ground by emphasizing values like love, justice, and dignity. Point out how patriarchal interpretations often conflict with these core biblical principles.

*Ask Thought-Provoking Questions*
Encourage critical thinking by asking questions like, "How does this interpretation align with Jesus' treatment of women?" or "What does this say about God's character?"

Building Coalitions

Building coalitions among diverse communities requires a focus on shared values of justice and liberation while honoring the unique perspectives and experiences of each group. Coalitions are powerful tools for systemic change, as they bring together a variety of skills, voices, and resources. However, uniting communities with different cultural, religious, and social backgrounds can be challenging. The key lies in fostering mutual respect, emphasizing common goals, and creating spaces for collaborative action.

*Identify Shared Values*
Start by identifying the values that unite diverse groups. Principles such as justice, equality, dignity, and compassion resonate across cultural and religious boundaries. These shared values form the foundation for coalition-building, providing common ground that transcends differences. For example, the biblical concept of loving one's neighbor (Luke 10:27) aligns with similar teachings in other traditions, such as the Quran's emphasis on mercy and the Buddhist principle of compassion. Highlighting these parallels fosters a sense of solidarity and shared purpose.

*Center on Specific Goals*
Coalitions thrive when they focus on clear, actionable goals. Identify specific issues, such as combating gender-based violence, addressing racial inequality, or advocating for economic justice, that align with the values of the coalition members. Defining tangible objectives helps keep the group focused and provides a roadmap for collaborative efforts. For instance, a coalition advocating for reproductive justice might unite faith-based organizations, feminist groups, and healthcare advocates around the shared goal of securing access to comprehensive reproductive healthcare.

*Create Inclusive Spaces*
Building coalitions requires creating spaces where all voices are heard and valued. This involves actively listening to the experiences and concerns of different groups, particularly those who have been historically marginalized. Recognize the intersections of oppression, such as how race, gender, class, and sexuality overlap, and ensure that the coalition's leadership and decision-making processes reflect this

diversity. By prioritizing inclusivity, coalitions can avoid replicating the very systems of inequality they seek to dismantle.

*Build Relationships Through Dialogue*
Fostering trust and understanding is essential for uniting diverse communities. Organize interfaith dialogues, cultural exchanges, or storytelling events where participants can share their experiences and learn from one another. These interactions help break down stereotypes, build empathy, and create a sense of collective identity. For example, an interfaith workshop on housing justice could feature testimonies from individuals directly impacted by housing discrimination, followed by collaborative discussions on solutions.

*Use Shared Symbols and Rituals*
Symbols and rituals can unite diverse communities by creating a sense of shared purpose and identity. For instance, lighting candles for justice, planting trees for environmental solidarity, or holding interfaith prayers for liberation can provide a spiritual and emotional anchor for coalition efforts. These practices affirm the coalition's shared values while respecting the distinct traditions of its members.

*Embrace Flexibility and Autonomy*
While coalitions work toward shared goals, it is important to respect the autonomy of each participating group. Allow space for members to pursue their own initiatives while contributing to the coalition's broader objectives. This flexibility prevents tension and ensures that the coalition remains a space of collaboration rather than coercion.

*Focus on Collective Wins*
Celebrate successes, no matter how small, to build momentum and maintain morale. Whether it's passing a piece of legislation, organizing a successful protest, or hosting a well-attended community event, acknowledging these victories reinforces the coalition's impact and inspires continued action.

The Ethics of Revolution - Lessons from the Past Revolutionary
Ethics

Revolutionary ethics grapples with the complex moral challenges that
arise in the pursuit of systemic change. Resistance to oppression is
often framed as a moral imperative, yet the methods and outcomes of
that resistance require careful reflection to ensure they align with the
principles of justice, equality, and dignity. Lessons from past
revolutions reveal that while the pursuit of liberation is vital, the
means of achieving it can either uphold or undermine the values that
inspired the struggle.

One central ethical challenge is balancing the urgency of action with
the integrity of purpose. Revolutionary movements often face intense
pressure to act decisively, but hasty or violent methods can risk
replicating the very structures of domination they seek to dismantle.
The French Revolution, for instance, began with the goal of liberty,
equality, and fraternity but descended into cycles of violence that
ultimately weakened its ideals. This raises critical questions: How can
resistance be effective without sacrificing its ethical foundation? What
methods truly dismantle oppression rather than replacing one form of
tyranny with another?

Another challenge lies in ensuring inclusivity and accountability
within revolutionary movements. History has shown that
marginalized groups, such as women, racial minorities, and
LGBTQ+ individuals, are often excluded from leadership roles or see
their needs sidelined in the broader revolutionary agenda. The civil
rights movement in the United States offers a powerful
counterexample, with leaders like Ella Baker emphasizing grassroots
organizing and collective leadership to create more equitable
structures.

Revolutionary ethics demands that resistance remain rooted in the
values it seeks to uphold. It calls for strategies that confront oppression
without perpetuating harm, emphasizing compassion, accountability,
and a commitment to building a future that reflects the principles of
justice and liberation. These lessons from the past remind us that how
we fight is as important as what we fight for.

Spiritual and Secular Synergy

Spiritual principles and secular strategies, often viewed as separate realms, can form a powerful synergy in effective activism. By combining the moral grounding and communal strength of spirituality with the practical, evidence-based approaches of secular activism, movements can address systemic oppression with a holistic and transformative approach.

*Shared Values as a Foundation*
Spiritual principles such as justice, compassion, and the inherent dignity of all people align closely with the goals of secular activism. These shared values provide a unifying foundation, bridging diverse communities. For example, the biblical mandate to "do justice, love kindness, and walk humbly" (Micah 6:8) resonates with human rights frameworks that emphasize equity and mutual respect.

*Sustained Energy through Hope*
Spirituality offers resilience and hope, essential for sustained activism. Movements rooted in spiritual practices often draw on rituals, prayers, or meditations to sustain energy and focus during long and challenging struggles. For instance, the civil rights movement relied on the church not just as an organizing hub but as a source of spiritual renewal, with songs, prayers, and sermons reinforcing the collective resolve to fight injustice.

*Strategic Action Grounded in Ethics*
Secular strategies such as nonviolent resistance, grassroots organizing, and policy advocacy are strengthened when paired with spiritual ethics that prioritize dignity and nonviolence. Gandhi's philosophy of *ahimsa* (nonviolence) and Martin Luther King Jr.'s adoption of nonviolent civil disobedience demonstrate how spiritual principles can guide effective, ethical resistance.

*Bridging Diverse Communities*
A synergy between spiritual and secular approaches can unite groups with different motivations but shared goals. Faith-based organizations can collaborate with secular advocacy groups on issues like environmental justice or gender equality, leveraging their combined resources, networks, and influence.

The Necessity of Resistance

The necessity of resistance against oppressive systems is not only a practical response to injustice but a profound moral imperative. Resistance is rooted in the belief that all people have inherent dignity and the right to live free from exploitation, inequality, and dehumanization. Insights from decolonization theory deepen this understanding, revealing how systemic oppression, whether through colonialism, patriarchy, or other power structures, requires active confrontation to dismantle the ideologies and systems that sustain it. Resistance is not optional; it is essential for justice, liberation, and the restoration of humanity's shared dignity.

Decolonization offers critical insights into the necessity of resistance by exposing how oppressive systems are constructed and maintained. Colonialism, for example, was not merely an act of physical domination but a process of cultural, spiritual, and psychological subjugation. Frantz Fanon, in *The Wretched of the Earth*, described how colonial systems dehumanized the colonized, stripping them of identity and agency while normalizing exploitation as inevitable. Fanon argued that resistance is not only a means of achieving liberation but also a process of reclaiming humanity and dignity. By rejecting the narratives imposed by oppressive systems, resistance disrupts the internalization of inferiority and asserts the inherent worth of the oppressed.

This imperative to resist is equally present in the struggle against patriarchy and other systemic injustices. Oppression thrives on silence and compliance, reinforcing hierarchies by convincing the marginalized that resistance is futile or unwarranted. Yet scripture, history, and contemporary struggles all affirm that resistance is not only justified but sacred. The story of the Hebrew midwives, Shiphrah and Puah (Exodus 1:15–21), demonstrates the moral necessity of defying unjust orders. Their refusal to carry out Pharaoh's edict to kill male Hebrew infants was an act of defiance rooted in their faith and commitment to justice, showing that resistance can be a form of profound spiritual conviction.

In the context of decolonization, resistance is also about dismantling the ideologies that uphold oppressive systems. This involves challenging not just explicit acts of domination but also the subtle ways these systems infiltrate culture, language, and thought. Decolonization is a process of reimagining and rebuilding, creating new systems and narratives that prioritize equity, inclusion, and justice. For instance, Indigenous movements around the world emphasize the importance of land reclamation and the restoration of traditional practices, not merely as acts of resistance but as affirmations of identity and sovereignty.

The moral imperative of resistance also requires addressing the intersections of various forms of oppression. Decolonization reminds us that systems like colonialism, patriarchy, racism, and capitalism are interconnected, often reinforcing one another. Effective resistance, therefore, must be intersectional, recognizing how these systems impact different groups uniquely and building coalitions that unite diverse communities in the fight for justice. For example, feminist decolonization movements highlight how colonialism and patriarchy have worked together to marginalize women, particularly women of color, and advocate for strategies that confront both simultaneously.

Challenging oppressive systems is not just about dismantling what is unjust but also about envisioning and building what is just. Resistance rooted in decolonization emphasizes the importance of hope and creativity, rejecting the inevitability of oppression and affirming the possibility of a liberated future. The vision of New Jerusalem in Revelation 21:1–4, where "there will be no more death or mourning or crying or pain," serves as a powerful metaphor for the ultimate goal of resistance: a world where justice and compassion prevail. This vision compels us to act, knowing that every step toward liberation is sacred and transformative.

Ultimately, the necessity of resistance is grounded in the moral truth that oppression cannot be tolerated. To resist is to affirm life, dignity, and the sacredness of all people. Insights from decolonization challenge us to confront not only external systems of oppression but also the internalized narratives that sustain them. Resistance, then, is both a moral duty and a profound act of faith in the possibility of a better world.

Pragmatism in Revolution

Pragmatism in revolution requires a clear understanding of power dynamics and the strategic use of resources, alliances, and timing to challenge oppression effectively. While moral imperatives often drive resistance, achieving meaningful change demands careful consideration of how power operates and how it can be confronted, redistributed, or dismantled. This balance between ideals and practicality is essential for ensuring that revolutionary efforts are both principled and impactful.

Power, in oppressive systems, is rarely concentrated in one place, it is diffused across political institutions, economic systems, cultural norms, and even interpersonal relationships. Pragmatic revolutionaries analyze these dynamics to identify vulnerabilities within the system. For instance, targeting economic structures that sustain oppression, such as exploitative labor practices, can weaken a regime's foundation without direct confrontation. Similarly, disrupting the cultural narratives that legitimize power, through art, education, or counter-narratives, can erode the social acceptance that sustains it.

Strategy is the bridge between revolutionary ideals and action. Effective movements prioritize achievable goals that build momentum while working toward broader systemic change. This involves identifying pressure points, key areas where targeted efforts can yield significant impact. Nonviolent movements, for example, often focus on symbolic actions, such as boycotts or sit-ins, to challenge power while minimizing harm. These strategies shift the focus from direct confrontation to creating moral and logistical dilemmas for those in power.

Coalition-building is another pragmatic necessity. Uniting diverse groups around shared objectives strengthens movements, but this requires navigating internal differences with transparency and respect. By balancing moral clarity with strategic flexibility, revolutionary movements can maintain integrity while adapting to complex realities, ensuring that their pursuit of justice is both principled and effective. Pragmatism, then, is not a compromise of ideals but a path to realizing them.

Balancing Ideals and Action

The tension between ethical ideals and the practical demands of
resistance is an enduring challenge for movements seeking justice and
liberation. While ethical principles provide the moral foundation for
resistance, the realities of confronting systemic oppression often
demand difficult choices and strategic compromises. Balancing these
two forces is essential for ensuring that resistance remains both
effective and aligned with its higher goals.

Ethical ideals serve as the compass for resistance, ensuring that the
pursuit of justice does not replicate the harm it seeks to undo. For
example, nonviolence is often embraced as a foundational principle
because it reflects the inherent dignity of all people, including those
complicit in oppression. However, the practical demands of resistance
may test this commitment, especially when faced with violence or
repression. Movements must grapple with the question: How can we
confront injustice decisively while remaining true to our values?

The practical demands of resistance often require flexibility and
adaptability. This might involve forming coalitions with groups that
have differing priorities, choosing tactics that may not fully reflect the
movement's ideals, or focusing on incremental change rather than
sweeping transformation. These decisions can create tension, as some
may perceive them as compromising core values. Yet, history shows
that pragmatic action often lays the groundwork for larger victories,
as seen in the civil rights movement's strategic use of legal challenges
and nonviolent protests to build momentum for systemic change.

Balancing ideals and action requires constant reflection, dialogue, and
accountability. Resistance movements must regularly evaluate
whether their strategies align with their ethical goals and make
adjustments when necessary. This balance ensures that resistance
remains not only effective but also transformative, embodying the
justice, equity, and compassion it seeks to achieve.

Lessons for Feminist Activism

The principles of balancing ideals and action offer crucial guidance for contemporary struggles for gender equality, where feminist activism often faces the dual challenge of staying true to its ethical foundations while navigating practical realities. By applying these lessons, feminist movements can confront systemic sexism effectively while maintaining the integrity of their vision for justice and equity.

*Upholding Inclusive Values*
Feminist activism must remain grounded in principles of inclusivity and intersectionality, ensuring that its strategies and goals address the diverse experiences of women, particularly those marginalized by race, class, sexuality, or ability. While prioritizing inclusivity may slow decision-making or complicate coalition-building, it prevents movements from replicating the exclusions they aim to dismantle.

*Strategic Pragmatism*
Practical demands often require feminist movements to choose battles wisely and adapt strategies. For instance, securing workplace protections or expanding reproductive rights might involve incremental policy changes rather than sweeping reforms. While this can feel like a compromise, such steps build momentum and lay the groundwork for larger systemic shifts. Feminist activism thrives when it pairs bold visions with achievable milestones.

*Coalition-Building Across Differences*
Uniting diverse groups with shared goals strengthens movements but demands thoughtful navigation of differing priorities. Collaborations with faith-based organizations on gender justice, for example, may require balancing secular feminist ideals with religious perspectives. Transparent dialogue and a focus on shared values ensure that coalitions amplify impact without compromising core feminist principles.

*Accountability and Reflection*
Regular reflection ensures strategies align with ethical goals. Movements must ask: Are we uplifting marginalized voices? Are our actions fostering genuine systemic change? This accountability keeps activism transformative and true to its mission.

Conclusion to Dragging the Patriarchy
Synthesis of Themes

The journey through "Dragging the Patriarchy" intertwines the principles of liberation theology, redefined worship, activism, and ethics into a unified framework for dismantling oppressive systems and building a world rooted in justice, equity, and inclusion. At its heart, this endeavor begins with liberation theology's insistence that faith is inseparable from justice. It challenges the idea that spirituality can exist in isolation from the lived realities of systemic oppression. Liberation theology compels us to view the divine as intimately present in the struggles of the marginalized, calling us to confront systems of power that perpetuate inequality. It reclaims scripture as a tool of resistance, offering narratives of empowerment and divine solidarity with the oppressed. Figures like the Hebrew midwives, Mary Magdalene, and the persistent widow emerge as icons of courage and agency, challenging patriarchal readings that have long silenced their voices. This theological lens affirms that dismantling patriarchy is not merely a social or political goal but a sacred imperative.

Redefining worship builds on this foundation, transforming sacred spaces into sites of resistance and empowerment. Traditional rituals often reflect and reinforce patriarchal hierarchies, but reimagined worship practices celebrate diversity, inclusion, and mutuality. Inclusive language for the divine, shared leadership roles, and rituals that honor the stories of marginalized groups transform worship into a living expression of liberation theology's principles. These redefined practices do more than critique existing structures; they actively construct new spaces where justice and equity are not only preached but enacted. Worship becomes a communal act of resistance, a celebration of diversity, and a source of spiritual sustenance for those engaged in the ongoing struggle for liberation.

Activism extends these principles into the public sphere, where the practical demands of resistance meet the ethical foundations of justice. Using scripture as a rhetorical and strategic tool, activists confront patriarchal systems with a moral authority that transcends politics. Passages like Amos 5:24, "Let justice roll on like a river," or Galatians 3:28, "There is neither male nor female, for you are all one in Christ Jesus," serve as rallying cries, linking contemporary struggles to timeless calls for equity and liberation. Activism rooted in this framework prioritizes inclusion and intersectionality, recognizing that the fight against patriarchy is interconnected with struggles against racism, classism, and other systems of oppression. By building coalitions across diverse communities and uniting around shared values, these movements amplify their impact and embody the collective power needed to create systemic change.

Ethics remains the guiding force, ensuring that resistance is both principled and effective. The tension between ideals and action is ever-present, requiring movements to navigate complex decisions while staying true to their core values. Revolutionary ethics demand that the means of resistance align with the desired ends, rejecting methods that replicate harm or exclusion. This ethical grounding insists that resistance be creative, compassionate, and accountable, drawing lessons from history to avoid the pitfalls of past revolutions. It challenges activists to imagine and build systems that reflect the justice and equity they seek, ensuring that the work of dismantling the old is accompanied by the creation of something better.

Together, these themes form a cohesive vision for dragging the patriarchy, a process of deconstruction and reconstruction that is spiritual, practical, and deeply transformative. Liberation theology provides the moral and theological foundation; redefined worship enacts these principles within sacred spaces; activism channels them into tangible efforts for systemic change; and ethics ensures that the process remains rooted in integrity and justice. This synthesis offers a blueprint for not only resisting patriarchal systems but also envisioning and building a world where the dignity and worth of all people are fully realized. It reminds us that this work is sacred, necessary, and profoundly hopeful, a testament to the possibility of liberation in both spiritual and material realms.

Reflections on the Journey

Reflecting on the transformative potential of applying the *F*ck the Patriarchy (FTP) lens to scripture and activism reveals a profound opportunity for personal and collective liberation. By reclaiming scripture as a living text of resistance and embedding it in the fight against systemic oppression, we not only challenge the patriarchal norms that have long dominated religious and societal structures but also create pathways for a more just and equitable world. This journey is about more than critique—it is about transformation, about envisioning new ways of being, worshiping, and acting that reflect the sacred dignity of all people.

The FTP lens turns scripture into a revolutionary tool, exposing its liberatory themes and using them to dismantle systems of injustice. It reframes stories long weaponized against women and marginalized groups, revealing their true power to inspire courage, agency, and resistance. Likewise, activism rooted in this framework draws strength from these reclaimed narratives, blending moral conviction with practical strategies to confront patriarchy in its many forms. The work of reimagining worship, building coalitions, and engaging with opponents becomes an act of sacred resistance, affirming that faith and justice are inseparable.

This reflection is not the end, it is a call to action. Readers are invited to take what they have learned and apply it to their own lives and communities. Organize workshops that reclaim scripture, create inclusive worship practices that center diverse voices, and use the moral clarity of biblical principles to challenge oppressive policies. Join or build coalitions that unite spiritual and secular forces in the fight for equity. This work begins with each of us, but its power lies in collective action.

The journey of dragging the patriarchy is ongoing, but with every step, we move closer to a world where justice and liberation are not ideals but realities.

Vision for the Future

Imagine a world where patriarchy is no longer the dominant force
shaping our lives, a world where justice, equity, and compassion
prevail. In this vision, power is no longer hoarded by the few but
shared among all, reflecting the inherent dignity and worth of every
individual. Women, long silenced or sidelined, stand as equal partners
in shaping communities, leading movements, and creating systems
that uplift rather than oppress. In this future, the stories and
experiences of the marginalized are not just heard but celebrated,
forming the foundation of a more inclusive and empathetic society.

This is a world where scripture is no longer a tool of control but a
source of liberation, its themes of justice and love reclaimed to inspire
courage and resilience. Worship spaces are transformed into
sanctuaries of inclusion, where all voices are valued, and rituals reflect
the diversity of human experience. Activism thrives as a sacred
practice, weaving together the spiritual and the practical to confront
oppression and create lasting change.

In this world, children grow up free from the constraints of gendered
expectations, taught instead to value empathy, collaboration, and
fairness. Communities thrive on mutual respect and solidarity,
addressing not only individual needs but systemic inequalities. The
dismantling of patriarchy has made room for new possibilities, systems
that prioritize collective well-being over domination, and relationships
built on partnership rather than hierarchy.

This vision is not a distant dream; it is a future we can begin to build
today. With every act of resistance, every coalition formed, and every
oppressive narrative challenged, we take a step closer to this reality.
Together, we can create a world where justice reigns and patriarchy
becomes a relic of the past, replaced by a society that truly reflects the
sacredness of all people.

# Part IV
*Collective Wisdom*

Introduction to Collective Wisdom Overview

Collective wisdom is the heartbeat of any transformative movement, and this chapter is a testament to the power of collaboration in reclaiming scripture and building a feminist theology that challenges patriarchy and fosters liberation. No single voice, perspective, or experience can fully encapsulate the breadth of what it means to dismantle systemic oppression and build a more just world. It is through the gathering of diverse voices, each shaped by unique histories, identities, and struggles, that the vision for a feminist theology rooted in justice and equity can truly flourish. This chapter seeks to embody that principle, presenting a tapestry of insights, reflections, and strategies from thinkers, theologians, activists, and community leaders who have contributed to the ongoing work of reclaiming the sacred for all people.

The concept of collective wisdom reflects the foundational belief that liberation is not an individual endeavor but a communal one. Feminist theology, in particular, thrives on this principle, emphasizing that theology must reflect the lived realities of diverse women and marginalized groups. It challenges the traditional notion of top-down theological authority, asserting instead that sacred truths emerge most authentically when shaped by those whose voices have historically been silenced or ignored. Collective wisdom allows us to draw from the strength and creativity of many, ensuring that our interpretations of scripture and visions for justice are richer, more inclusive, and more transformative than any one perspective could achieve alone.

Reclaiming scripture through the lens of collective wisdom means centering the stories, experiences, and insights of women and other marginalized groups. These voices bring to light the hidden threads of resistance, courage, and agency within biblical narratives, challenging patriarchal readings that have sought to erase or distort them. For example, the reinterpretation of Eve as a seeker of knowledge, or Mary Magdalene as a leader and witness, emerges from feminist scholars and communities who dared to see these stories through a different lens. Their collective work reclaims these figures not as symbols of subjugation but as icons of empowerment, offering inspiration for those who continue to resist oppression today.

This chapter also highlights the importance of intergenerational and pluralistic collaboration. The wisdom of elders, who have witnessed decades of struggle and progress, enriches the movement with historical context and hard-earned insights. Meanwhile, the voices of younger generations bring fresh perspectives, innovation, and a refusal to accept the limitations of the past. Together, they form a dynamic dialogue that propels feminist theology forward, ensuring it remains relevant and responsive to the evolving challenges of our time. Intersectionality, too, is critical, as it recognizes that gender oppression does not exist in isolation but intersects with race, class, sexuality, ability, and other forms of marginalization. Collective wisdom demands that these intersecting realities be at the forefront of our theological work, creating a framework that is inclusive and justice-oriented.

Beyond reclaiming scripture, collective wisdom also informs how we build communities and movements. It challenges hierarchical models of leadership and decision-making, emphasizing collaboration, mutual support, and shared power. This approach not only reflects the values of feminist theology but also models the kind of world we seek to create, a world where justice and equity are not just ideals but lived realities. By listening to and learning from one another, we create a space where every voice matters and where the work of liberation is strengthened by the contributions of all.

As we embark on this exploration of collective wisdom, let us remember that this chapter is not merely about reflection, it is a call to action. It invites readers to embrace collaboration in their own lives, to seek out diverse perspectives, and to contribute their own voices to the ongoing work of reclaiming scripture and building feminist theology. Together, we can harness the transformative power of collective wisdom to challenge patriarchy, reimagine the sacred, and create a more just and inclusive world.

Voices of the Resistance
Essays and Reflections from Feminist Theologians

The voices of feminist theologians have reshaped the way we engage with scripture, transforming it from a tool often wielded to justify oppression into a source of resistance and liberation. These theologians challenge patriarchal interpretations of sacred texts, reclaiming their transformative potential and positioning scripture as a powerful ally in the fight for justice. Their essays and reflections illuminate the ways scripture can speak to the struggles of today, offering both critique of systemic oppression and inspiration for resistance.

Elisabeth Schüssler Fiorenza, a pioneer in feminist biblical scholarship, emphasizes the importance of reading scripture with a "hermeneutic of suspicion." She argues that traditional interpretations of the Bible have been shaped by patriarchal agendas, often silencing or marginalizing women's voices and experiences. In her groundbreaking work, *In Memory of Her*, Fiorenza reclaims the role of women in the early Christian movement, particularly Mary Magdalene, whom she identifies as a leader and apostle. Her work challenges the erasure of women's contributions to Christianity, inviting readers to see the Bible not as a monolith of patriarchal thought but as a collection of diverse voices, many of which speak to the realities of resistance and liberation.

Phyllis Trible, another influential feminist theologian, reframes biblical narratives to highlight their liberatory potential. In her essay collection *Texts of Terror*, Trible explores the stories of women in scripture who have suffered violence and oppression, such as Hagar, Tamar, and the unnamed concubine in Judges 19. While these stories are often painful and difficult, Trible's analysis reveals their power to expose the realities of systemic violence and to call for justice. By giving voice to these women, she challenges readers to confront the ways scripture has been used to perpetuate harm and to seek new interpretations that honor the dignity and humanity of all people.

Letty M. Russell, a theologian deeply committed to liberation and inclusion, focuses on scripture as a communal text that calls for action. In her work *Church in the Round*, Russell advocates for an egalitarian vision of faith communities, grounded in mutuality and shared leadership. She draws on stories like that of the persistent widow in Luke 18, who demands justice from an indifferent judge, as an example of how scripture inspires resilience and advocacy. Russell's reflections encourage us to view scripture not as a static set of rules but as a living dialogue that speaks to the realities of struggle and the possibilities of liberation.

Renita J. Weems brings an intersectional perspective to feminist theology, exploring the intersections of race, gender, and faith in her writings. In works like *Just a Sister Away*, Weems examines the relationships between women in the Bible, such as Hagar and Sarah, uncovering the complexities of power, pain, and solidarity. Her reflections reveal how scripture mirrors the tensions and possibilities of human relationships, offering insights into how women can navigate systems of oppression while building communities of mutual support and empowerment.

Feminist theologians also emphasize the importance of reimagining the language we use to talk about God. Scholars like Rosemary Radford Ruether challenge the exclusively patriarchal imagery of God as "Father" or "King," advocating for metaphors that reflect the diversity and inclusivity of the divine. This reimagining not only challenges theological hierarchies but also empowers those who have been excluded from traditional faith narratives to see themselves as sacred and valued.

These voices of resistance remind us that reclaiming scripture is not simply an academic exercise, it is a deeply political and spiritual act. By uncovering the liberatory themes within scripture, feminist theologians provide tools for confronting oppression and inspiring action. Their work invites us to read the Bible with fresh eyes, to challenge patriarchal interpretations, and to embrace scripture as a source of courage, agency, and hope. These reflections are both a call to resistance and a testament to the transformative power of collective wisdom in the ongoing struggle for justice.

Themes of Empowerment

Key themes of empowerment, agency, liberation, and community building, lie at the heart of feminist theology and its reclamation of scripture as a tool for justice. These themes challenge patriarchal narratives that have historically silenced marginalized voices and instead offer a transformative vision of faith as a source of strength, resilience, and collective action.

Agency is central to empowering individuals within the context of faith. Feminist theologians highlight stories where women in scripture exercise their agency, defying societal norms and asserting their autonomy. Figures like Deborah, a judge and prophet, or the persistent widow in Luke 18, embody courage and determination, showing that agency is not only possible but sacred. These narratives inspire individuals to see themselves as active participants in their own liberation, capable of challenging systems that seek to oppress.

Liberation is a foundational theme, connecting personal and systemic freedom. Feminist theology draws on narratives like the Exodus story, where God's liberating power is revealed in the Israelites' journey from slavery to freedom. This theme transcends individual struggles, addressing systemic issues like sexism, racism, and economic inequality. Liberation reminds us that faith is not about submission but about challenging unjust structures and envisioning a world rooted in justice and equity.

Community building reflects the understanding that empowerment is not achieved in isolation but through collaboration and mutual support. The New Testament's emphasis on early Christian communities as spaces of sharing, inclusion, and collective care inspires feminist theologians to reimagine faith communities as places where everyone's voice is valued. Community is both the means and the goal of empowerment, fostering solidarity in the struggle for justice.

Together, these themes affirm that scripture, reclaimed, becomes a source of hope, resilience, and transformative power for individuals and communities alike.

Activists and Community Leaders Speak

Activists and grassroots leaders have long drawn on scripture to ground their work in justice, resilience, and moral clarity. By reclaiming sacred texts as tools of empowerment, these individuals bridge faith and activism, using scripture to inspire communities, challenge systems of oppression, and build movements for equity and inclusion.

Sojourner Truth, an abolitionist and women's rights advocate, famously invoked scripture to challenge both racial and gender inequalities. In her speech "Ain't I a Woman?" she used the biblical story of Eve to argue for women's strength and capacity, flipping patriarchal interpretations on their head. Her rhetorical use of scripture gave her arguments moral weight, inspiring action against systemic oppression.

Oscar Romero, the martyred archbishop of El Salvador, is another powerful example. Romero drew heavily on the prophetic tradition of scripture, quoting passages like Isaiah 10:1–2, "Woe to those who make unjust laws," to denounce systemic poverty and political violence. His sermons became rallying cries for the oppressed, blending spiritual conviction with demands for structural change.

In the United States, Rev. William Barber, leader of the Poor People's Campaign, uses scripture to address systemic inequality and advocate for justice. Citing passages such as Amos 5:24, "Let justice roll on like a river," he mobilizes faith communities to confront economic injustice, racial discrimination, and environmental degradation.

At the grassroots level, leaders in Indigenous communities have drawn on scripture to support land rights and environmental justice. Many connect biblical themes of stewardship and creation care to their activism, challenging policies that exploit natural resources and harm marginalized communities.

These activists and leaders exemplify how scripture, when reclaimed as a tool for justice, can inspire transformative action, providing hope and moral grounding for the work of liberation.

The Feminist Canon Empowering Biblical Passages

The Bible, when read through a feminist lens, reveals powerful themes of resistance and empowerment that have inspired individuals and movements across generations.

Exodus 1:15–21 – The Defiance of Shiphrah and Puah
This passage highlights the courage of the Hebrew midwives, Shiphrah and Puah, who defy Pharaoh's orders to kill male Hebrew infants. Their civil disobedience, rooted in their reverence for God, saves countless lives and sets the stage for the liberation of the Israelites. This story affirms that resistance to oppression is a sacred act and that women's courage can change the course of history.

Judges 4–5 – Deborah's Leadership
Deborah, a prophet and judge, exemplifies empowered leadership in a patriarchal society. She leads Israel to victory over its oppressors, demonstrating wisdom, courage, and authority. Deborah's story challenges traditional gender roles and affirms women's ability to lead with strength and conviction.

Luke 8:1–3 – Women Supporting Jesus' Ministry
This passage highlights the often-overlooked role of women as key supporters of Jesus' ministry. Figures like Mary Magdalene, Joanna, and Susanna are named as leaders and financial backers, affirming that women have always been integral to faith communities. Their inclusion underscores the importance of women's contributions and challenges their erasure in patriarchal interpretations.

Galatians 3:28 – Radical Equality in Christ
Paul's declaration that "there is neither Jew nor Gentile, neither slave nor free, nor is there male and female, for you are all one in Christ Jesus" provides a foundational vision of equality. This verse has been a cornerstone for feminist theology, affirming the radical inclusivity of the Gospel and challenging systems of hierarchy and oppression.

Luke 18:1–8 – The Persistent Widow
In this parable, Jesus tells the story of a widow who demands justice from an indifferent judge, eventually wearing him down with her persistence. This narrative celebrates resilience and advocacy, showing that even the most marginalized individuals can enact

change through steadfast action. It's a call to persist in the fight for justice, even against overwhelming odds.

Proverbs 31:10–31 – The Virtuous Woman
While often co-opted to confine women to domestic roles, this passage, when reexamined, highlights the entrepreneurial, independent, and strong qualities of the "virtuous woman." She is a provider, a decision-maker, and a leader in her community, challenging traditional notions of subservience and dependence.

John 20:11–18 – Mary Magdalene as Witness to the Resurrection
Mary Magdalene's role as the first witness to the resurrection and messenger to the apostles positions her as a central figure in the Christian narrative. This passage affirms women's spiritual authority and challenges patriarchal attempts to diminish their roles in faith communities.

Isaiah 61:1–3 – Proclaiming Liberation
This prophetic passage, later echoed by Jesus in Luke 4, proclaims good news to the poor, freedom for the oppressed, and comfort for those who mourn. It provides a powerful framework for liberation theology, affirming that justice and healing are central to God's vision for humanity.

Ruth 1:16–17 – Ruth's Loyalty and Strength
Ruth's declaration to Naomi, "Where you go, I will go," reflects deep loyalty, courage, and solidarity. Her story is a testament to the power of women's relationships and their capacity to support one another through hardship and uncertainty.

Matthew 5:13–16 – The Light of the World
Jesus' call for his followers to be "the light of the world" affirms the power of individuals and communities to create positive change. This passage encourages believers to embody justice and compassion, illuminating the path toward a more equitable world.

Reinterpretations for Today

Reimagining biblical passages through a modern lens connects their timeless themes of justice and empowerment to contemporary struggles, offering fresh insights and renewed inspiration for those working to dismantle systemic oppression and build a more equitable world. Below are reinterpretations of key passages, emphasizing their relevance to today's fights for justice.

Exodus 1:15–21 – Shiphrah and Puah's Defiance
In today's world, Shiphrah and Puah can be seen as symbols of resistance to unjust laws and policies, such as those targeting immigrants, reproductive rights, or marginalized communities. Their refusal to comply with Pharaoh's genocidal decree is a call to civil disobedience in the face of systemic injustice.

Judges 4–5 – Deborah's Leadership
Deborah's story resonates with the ongoing struggle for women's leadership in politics, business, and religious institutions. Her role as a prophet and judge challenges gender stereotypes and affirms that women possess the wisdom and authority to lead transformative movements.

Luke 8:1–3 – Women Supporting Jesus' Ministry
This passage reminds us that women have always been integral to the work of justice and liberation. In modern contexts, it highlights the critical roles women play in activism, philanthropy, and community-building, often without recognition. It challenges society to acknowledge and honor women's contributions as indispensable to movements for change.

Galatians 3:28 – Radical Equality in Christ
Paul's declaration of equality is a powerful affirmation for today's struggles against intersectional oppression. It speaks to the necessity of dismantling systems that privilege certain identities over others, whether based on race, gender, class, or sexuality.

Luke 18:1–8 – The Persistent Widow
The widow's persistence mirrors the resilience of activists fighting systemic injustices like voter suppression, gender-based violence, or environmental degradation. Her refusal to accept apathy or

corruption from the judge resonates with those who demand accountability from leaders and institutions. This story inspires modern movements to persist, even when progress feels slow or resistance seems overwhelming.

Proverbs 31:10–31 – The Virtuous Woman
Reexamining this passage reveals a portrait of a woman who is independent, resourceful, and impactful in her community. For today's feminist movements, the "virtuous woman" challenges traditional domestic ideals and celebrates women as entrepreneurs, leaders, and agents of social change.

John 20:11–18 – Mary Magdalene as Witness
Mary Magdalene's role as the first to witness the resurrection affirms women's spiritual and leadership authority. Today, her story empowers women in faith communities to reclaim their rightful roles as preachers, teachers, and leaders, challenging patriarchal structures that seek to limit their voices.

Isaiah 61:1–3 – Proclaiming Liberation
This prophetic call to action resonates with modern movements for justice, such as Black Lives Matter, climate activism, and the fight for LGBTQ+ rights. It underscores the sacredness of advocating for the oppressed, comforting those who suffer, and working to dismantle systems of harm.

Ruth 1:16–17 – Ruth's Loyalty
Ruth's unwavering commitment to Naomi symbolizes solidarity across differences. Today, it calls us to allyship in struggles for justice, urging privileged groups to stand with marginalized communities in dismantling systemic inequalities. Ruth's loyalty reminds us that liberation is collective and requires deep, lasting commitments.

Matthew 5:13–16 – The Light of the World
Jesus' call to be a light resonates with activists who shine a spotlight on injustice and illuminate paths to equity. It challenges individuals and communities to lead by example, embodying values of compassion and justice in ways that inspire others to join the work of transformation.

Building a Toolkit for Resistance

Building a toolkit for resistance involves turning the curated passages into actionable resources for activism, worship, and personal reflection. These practical approaches allow readers to integrate scripture's empowering messages into their efforts to challenge oppression and build a more just world.

Activism: Amplifying Justice

*Public Speeches and Protests*: Use passages like Amos 5:24 ("Let justice roll on like a river") or Luke 18:1–8 (the persistent widow) in speeches or on protest signs to inspire moral urgency and resilience. These texts frame activism as a sacred act and a call to accountability for unjust systems.

*Advocacy Campaigns*: Incorporate texts like Isaiah 61:1–3 ("proclaim good news to the poor") into campaigns for economic justice or marginalized communities. Tie their themes to policy demands, showing how scripture aligns with the movement's goals.

*Community Organizing:* Anchor organizing meetings with reflections on passages like Ruth 1:16–17, emphasizing solidarity and mutual commitment in the fight for justice.

Worship: Creating Sacred Spaces for Resistance

*Rituals and Services*: Design services that center passages like John 20:11–18 (Mary Magdalene's leadership) to affirm women's roles in faith and leadership. Use candle-lighting rituals or collective prayers to highlight scripture's liberatory themes.

*Music and Art*: Incorporate hymns or visual art inspired by texts like Matthew 5:13–16 (light of the world) to foster hope and inspire action.

Personal Reflection: Cultivating Inner Strength

*Meditation and Journaling*: Reflect on passages like Galatians 3:28 to explore personal experiences of identity and justice. Use journaling prompts to connect scripture to your struggles and goals.

*Affirmations*: Turn empowering verses into daily affirmations, reminding yourself of your agency and role in creating change.

This toolkit ensures scripture becomes a living resource, driving action and nurturing resilience.

Closing Reflections

The journey through collective wisdom reveals a profound truth: the power to create a just and equitable world lies not in the hands of one individual but in the shared strength of many. By coming together, weaving diverse voices and experiences into a unified effort, we amplify our capacity to challenge oppression and imagine transformative possibilities. Collective wisdom honors the sacred value of each person's story, recognizing that liberation is a shared endeavor, shaped by collaboration, mutual respect, and the courage to dismantle the systems that divide us.

Through the voices of theologians, activists, and community leaders, we see the transformative potential of reclaiming scripture and redefining faith. These contributions remind us that justice is not an abstract ideal but a lived practice, one rooted in empathy, resilience, and action. By embracing collective wisdom, we challenge the isolating narratives of individualism and scarcity, replacing them with a vision of abundance and solidarity. We affirm that each voice, no matter how small it may seem, carries the potential to shift systems, inspire change, and build a foundation for liberation.

This work is not easy, nor is it swift. But collective wisdom reminds us that we do not do it alone. In every step we take toward justice, we carry with us the insights, struggles, and victories of those who came before us and those who walk alongside us. Together, we reimagine what is possible, transforming faith into a dynamic force for healing and equity. The collective power of wisdom is not just a tool for resistance, it is the blueprint for a world where all can thrive. Let this understanding guide and sustain us as we continue the sacred work of justice and liberation.

# Conclusion

Call to Action Owning Spiritual Narratives

Reclaiming and reinterpreting spiritual narratives is an act of liberation, a refusal to accept the patriarchal constraints that have long shaped how women understand and express their faith. For centuries, women's voices have been silenced or marginalized in religious spaces, their stories misinterpreted or erased by traditions and systems that prioritize male authority. This call to action invites women to break free from these constraints, to own their spiritual journeys with courage and authenticity, and to reclaim the sacred narratives that affirm their dignity, agency, and leadership.

To begin this work, women must first recognize the ways patriarchal structures have distorted their spiritual experiences. Traditional interpretations of scripture often reduce women to passive figures, defined by their relationships to men or their adherence to rigid roles. Eve is labeled the archetypal sinner, Mary Magdalene the repentant woman, and the Proverbs 31 woman an impossible ideal of domestic virtue. These interpretations not only limit women's understanding of their spiritual worth but also reinforce societal norms that confine them to roles of submission and service. Reclaiming these narratives means challenging these distortions and uncovering the liberatory themes that patriarchal readings have suppressed.

Owning one's spiritual narrative also involves reimagining scripture as a living, dynamic text that speaks to women's lived experiences. Women are invited to see themselves in the courage of Shiphrah and Puah, the resilience of Ruth, the leadership of Deborah, and the wisdom of Mary Magdalene. These figures are not relics of the past but role models for modern faith, examples of women who defied norms, led movements, and claimed their place in the sacred story. By embracing these narratives, women can draw strength and inspiration to confront the challenges of today, whether they are breaking glass ceilings, resisting systemic oppression, or leading communities toward justice.

Reinterpreting spiritual journeys also requires women to reclaim their relationship with the divine. For too long, patriarchal theology has presented God in exclusively masculine terms, reinforcing hierarchies that diminish women's spiritual authority. Reclaiming this relationship involves embracing inclusive and expansive language for the divine—God as Creator, Nurturer, Wisdom, or Spirit—that reflects the diversity of human experience. This shift empowers women to see themselves as sacred, as reflections of the divine, and as equal partners in the ongoing work of creation and justice.

Breaking free from patriarchal constraints is not only a personal journey but also a communal act. Women reclaiming their spiritual narratives often find strength and solidarity in sharing their stories with others. Faith communities that center women's voices and experiences become spaces of healing and empowerment, where individuals can support one another in their journeys and collectively challenge oppressive systems. These communities embody the vision of "church in the round," where power is shared, stories are celebrated, and liberation is the guiding principle.

This call to action is about more than resistance—it is about creation. By owning their spiritual narratives, women not only reject the constraints of the past but also build a future where faith is a source of empowerment rather than oppression. This work requires courage, reflection, and a willingness to challenge entrenched norms, but the rewards are profound: a faith that reflects women's experiences, a theology that uplifts rather than diminishes, and a spiritual journey that is fully one's own.

To every woman reading this, the invitation is clear: Reclaim your voice, your story, your connection to the divine. See yourself not as a follower of tradition but as a creator of it, shaping a spirituality that reflects your truth and the truth of justice and liberation. This is your sacred journey, own it boldly and unapologetically. Together, let us create a faith that is as expansive, inclusive, and transformative as the world we envision.

Practical Steps for Engagement

Using scripture as a source of empowerment in daily life and activism requires intentional engagement, reflection, and application. By reclaiming its liberatory messages and integrating them into both personal and public spheres, individuals can draw strength and inspiration for challenging oppression and building justice.

*Reflect on Empowering Texts*
Identify passages that resonate with themes of justice, courage, and agency, such as Galatians 3:28, Luke 18:1–8, or Exodus 1:15–21. Meditate on these texts regularly, journaling about how they connect to your experiences and the challenges you face. Use this time to reaffirm your commitment to justice and envision how these narratives inspire your actions.

*Create Affirmations*
Turn empowering scripture into daily affirmations. For example, "I am the light of the world" (Matthew 5:14) or "I am called to act justly, love mercy, and walk humbly" (Micah 6:8). Repeat these phrases in moments of doubt or struggle to remind yourself of your strength and purpose.

*Integrate Scripture into Activism*
Use scripture in speeches, protests, or advocacy campaigns to amplify calls for justice. Incorporate verses like Isaiah 61:1–3 or Amos 5:24 into messaging that demands accountability and systemic change. These texts connect activism to a broader moral and spiritual framework.

*Foster Community Engagement*
Organize small groups or workshops to explore scripture as a tool for liberation. Discuss how specific passages challenge oppressive norms and inspire collective action. Create rituals that affirm participants' voices and celebrate their shared commitment to justice.

*Advocate for Inclusive Worship*
Encourage faith communities to embrace inclusive interpretations of scripture. Highlight women's stories and diverse perspectives during services to reflect the richness of the sacred text.

# Additional Resources

The journey of reclaiming scripture and dismantling patriarchal theology is deeply enriched by engaging with the work of feminist theologians, organizations, and resources that have paved the way for spiritual empowerment and liberation. Below is a curated list of key texts, organizations, and tools that can guide and inspire those committed to this work.

Begin with the foundational works of feminist theology, where scholars have challenged traditional interpretations of scripture and offered new lenses through which to view faith. Books such as "In Memory of Her" by Elisabeth Schüssler Fiorenza and "She Who Is" by Elizabeth A. Johnson are essential reading for understanding the historical and theological foundations of feminist critiques of Christianity. Fiorenza's work is particularly significant for its exploration of early Christian communities, where women often held positions of leadership that were later erased by institutional patriarchy. Johnson's text reclaims the concept of God as feminine, challenging deeply entrenched masculine imagery that has dominated Christian theology.

"The Dance of the Dissident Daughter" by Sue Monk Kidd is another transformative text that chronicles the author's personal journey from patriarchal Christianity to a spirituality rooted in feminist principles. For readers interested in liberation theology with a feminist perspective, "Womanist Theology" by Delores S. Williams offers a crucial intersectional approach, addressing the unique spiritual and social struggles of Black women within religious contexts. Pairing this with the groundbreaking "Sisters in the Wilderness" by Delores S. Williams deepens the understanding of how scripture speaks to the lived experiences of marginalized women.

For those seeking texts that incorporate a global perspective, "Feminist Theology from the Third World" edited by Ursula King brings together voices from diverse cultures, showing how feminist theology intersects with issues of colonialism, race, and global inequality. Kwok Pui-lan's "Postcolonial Imagination and Feminist Theology" is an essential addition to this conversation, examining how colonial histories have shaped theological discourse and how reclaiming spirituality can also act as a form of decolonization.

The work of queer theologians also plays a vital role in expanding the conversation around inclusivity and liberation within religious spaces. "Radical Love: An Introduction to Queer Theology" by Patrick S. Cheng and "Queer Theology: Beyond Apologetics" by Gerard Loughlin challenge readers to embrace a more inclusive and liberatory understanding of scripture. For those wanting to dive deeper into the intersections of gender, sexuality, and spirituality, "Omnigender" by Virginia Ramey Mollenkott offers profound insights.

Organizations dedicated to feminist theology and activism provide invaluable support and resources for those looking to engage with like-minded communities. The Women's Ordination Conference advocates for the full inclusion of women in ordained ministry within the Catholic Church, challenging centuries of patriarchal exclusion. Similarly, Women of the Wall is an interfaith organization that fights for gender equality within Jewish worship practices. Their work underscores the global nature of the struggle against religious patriarchy.

For interfaith feminist activism, The Feminist Studies in Religion organization serves as a hub for scholarly and community-based work, publishing the Journal of Feminist Studies in Religion, which explores critical issues in theology and praxis. The Reclaiming Tradition movement, rooted in feminist spirituality, provides resources for creating inclusive rituals and empowering worship practices that celebrate diversity and equality.

In practical terms, tools like Bible study guides written from a feminist perspective can be transformative for personal and community engagement with scripture. "The Women's Bible Commentary" edited by Carol A. Newsom and Sharon H. Ringe offers critical insights into biblical texts, reframing them through feminist and intersectional lenses. For younger audiences or those new to these ideas, books like "A New Christian Manifesto" by Bob Ekblad can serve as an accessible introduction to using scripture for activism and social justice.

Digital resources have also become increasingly important for feminist theological exploration. Websites such as Feminist Theology Online and The Women's Lectionary Project offer free articles, liturgical resources, and commentary designed to support the work of inclusive worship and theological study. Podcasts like "The Liturgists Podcast", "Queerology", and "The Bible for Normal People" provide engaging discussions that challenge traditional readings of scripture while exploring feminist and queer approaches to faith.

Community tools and group-based initiatives also play a vital role in sustaining this work. Establishing or joining feminist scripture study groups allows individuals to collectively explore and reinterpret sacred texts, fostering dialogue and solidarity. Organizations like Sojourners, which focuses on faith-based social justice, provide frameworks for connecting theological reflection with activism.

In addition to theological texts, works of fiction and memoir can illuminate the intersection of spirituality and feminism in unique and accessible ways. Sue Monk Kidd's "The Book of Longings", a fictional account of the life of Jesus' imagined wife, offers a profound meditation on women's voices and agency in religious narratives. Similarly, "Untamed" by Glennon Doyle weaves personal stories with reflections on faith, feminism, and liberation.

Finally, activism rooted in feminist theology requires tools for reflection and resilience. Practices like journaling, meditation, and creative expression can help sustain spiritual growth and liberation. Incorporating feminist reinterpretations of scripture into daily prayer or community worship can transform these practices into acts of rebellion and empowerment.

The journey of reclaiming scripture and dismantling patriarchy is a deeply personal and collective endeavor. These resources, texts, organizations, and tools, serve as companions and guides for those willing to challenge the status quo, embrace new interpretations, and build a more just and equitable spiritual community. Through engagement with these works and communities, women and allies can find strength, solidarity, and inspiration to continue the fight for liberation.

# Curated Passages

Genesis 3:1-7 – Eve as the First Rebel, Not the First Sinner
Original: Eve eats the fruit from the tree of knowledge of good and
evil, traditionally interpreted as the origin of sin.

Reinterpretation: Eve's act of eating the fruit is an act of courage and
agency. She chooses knowledge over ignorance, challenging the limits
imposed upon her. Rather than a sinner, she becomes a symbol of
liberation, seeking truth and understanding even in the face of divine
authority. This reinterpretation invites us to embrace the pursuit of
knowledge and challenge systems that rely on enforced ignorance.

Exodus 15:20-21 – Miriam's Song of Liberation
Original: Miriam leads the women in song and dance after the
Israelites cross the Red Sea.

Reinterpretation: Miriam is a leader of liberation, celebrating
liberation from oppression and inspiring her community to rejoice in
their collective strength. Her song is not merely a moment of triumph
but a rallying cry for ongoing liberation against all forms of
enslavement. This passage reminds us of the power of women's voices
and leadership in movements for justice.

Luke 10:38-42 – Mary and Martha
Original: Mary is praised for sitting at Jesus' feet while Martha is
criticized for being too focused on domestic work.

Reinterpretation: Rather than pitting the sisters against each other,
this passage highlights the importance of balance. Mary's choice to
learn and engage in theological discourse challenges societal norms
that confined women to domestic roles, while Martha's labor reflects
the unseen work that sustains communities. Together, they represent
the multifaceted contributions of women to spiritual and communal
life.

John 4:7-30 – The Samaritan Woman at the Well
Original: Jesus speaks to a Samaritan woman, breaking social and
gender boundaries.

Reinterpretation: The Samaritan woman becomes a symbol of empowerment, engaging in theological dialogue with Jesus and ultimately becoming a messenger to her community. Her story emphasizes the breaking of barriers and the inclusion of marginalized voices in spiritual leadership. It is a call to challenge exclusionary practices and uplift those on the margins.

Revelation 21:1-4 – A New Heaven and a New Earth
Original: A vision of the end of suffering and the establishment of God's kingdom.

Reinterpretation: This passage becomes a blueprint for hope and transformation, envisioning a world free from oppression, violence, and inequality. It is not merely a promise of future redemption but a call to action for creating a just and equitable society in the here and now. It inspires resilience and collective effort to build a better world.

Psalm 22:1-5 – A Prayer for Strength in Struggle
Original: A lament of abandonment and a plea for deliverance.

Reinterpretation: The Psalmist's cry becomes a prayer for those enduring oppression, expressing both the pain of suffering and the hope for liberation. It is a reminder that faith can coexist with struggle and that voicing pain is an act of liberation against systems that demand silence.

Romans 16:1-7 – Honoring Women Leaders
Original: Paul acknowledges women like Phoebe, Junia, and others as leaders in the early church.

Reinterpretation: This passage highlights the integral role of women in the early Christian movement, challenging interpretations that erase or diminish their contributions. It serves as a reminder of the historical precedent for women's leadership in spiritual communities and a call to restore and honor that legacy today.

# Strategies and Frameworks for Activism

Deconstructing Patriarchal Narratives
Strategy: Identify and critique traditional interpretations of scripture that reinforce patriarchy.
*Example*: Reinterpret Eve's narrative in Genesis as an act of agency and knowledge-seeking, rather than the origin of sin.
Application: Use feminist exegesis to uncover the historical and cultural contexts of problematic passages, revealing their constructed nature.
Key Practice: Host Bible study groups focused on exploring alternative readings of traditionally oppressive texts.

Reclaiming Sacred Texts
Strategy: Highlight empowering stories in scripture and elevate overlooked figures.
*Example*: Celebrate Mary Magdalene as a leader and witness to the resurrection, challenging efforts to diminish her role.
Application: Create resources (e.g., guides, sermons, or workshops) that showcase reimagined biblical narratives, emphasizing themes of liberation and liberation.
Key Practice: Integrate reinterpreted scripture into worship, prayer, and community discussions.

Building Women's Liberation Theology
Framework: Combine spiritual empowerment with political action to challenge systemic oppression.
*Principle 1*: Faith should inspire action for justice and equity.
*Principle 2*: Center the voices of marginalized women in theological discourse.
Application: Develop feminist liberation theology frameworks tailored to your community's needs, drawing on both scripture and lived experiences.
Key Practice: Collaborate with local organizations to link theological study with grassroots activism.

Redefining Worship and Ritual
Strategy: Create inclusive, feminist worship practices that celebrate diversity and dismantle exclusionary norms.

*Example*: Design rituals that honor women's contributions in scripture and modern activism.
Application: Adapt traditional liturgies to reflect progressive values, including gender-neutral language and participatory elements.
Key Practice: Host interfaith gatherings that focus on shared principles of equality, justice, and compassion.

Activating the FTP Lens
Framework: Use the "FTP (F*ck the Patriarchy)" lens to critique and resist power structures.
*Principle 1*: Patriarchy is a constructed system, not a divine mandate.
*Principle 2*: Scripture can be a weapon for liberation, not chains.
Application: Deploy the FTP lens in activism by using biblical rhetoric to critique authoritarian policies and highlight calls for justice in scripture.
Key Practice: Write and deliver speeches, articles, or sermons that use scripture to challenge systemic injustice.

Leveraging Biblical Language in Activism
Strategy: Reappropriate biblical themes and language to inspire liberation and solidarity.
*Example*: Use passages like Galatians 3:28 ("There is neither male nor female…") to advocate for gender equality.
Application: Incorporate reimagined scripture into campaigns, protests, and public dialogues to mobilize communities around shared spiritual values.
Key Practice: Collaborate with allies across faith traditions to build interfaith coalitions for change.

Community Building and Collective Action
Framework: Foster solidarity by linking theological study with practical activism.
*Principle 1*: Liberation is collective, not individual.
*Principle 2*: Communities are stronger when they amplify diverse voices and experiences.
Application: Organize study groups, workshops, and events that connect scripture with real-world issues, such as reproductive rights, racial justice, and LGBTQ+ inclusion.
Key Practice: Partner with feminist theologians, activists, and local organizations to create spaces for dialogue and action.

Balancing Ethics and Strategy
Framework: Integrate the ethical insights of liberation theology with the pragmatic strategies.
*Principle 1*: Effective liberation requires both moral clarity and tactical acumen.
*Principle 2*: Revolution is justified when it dismantles oppressive systems.
Application: Develop action plans that prioritize justice and inclusivity while navigating the realities of power dynamics.
Key Practice: Use community forums to discuss the balance between idealism and pragmatism in activism.

Sustaining Liberation through Spiritual Practices
Strategy: Incorporate rituals and practices that nurture resilience and hope.
*Example*: Use Psalms of lament and protest as prayers for courage and solidarity.
Application: Create spaces for collective reflection and healing, such as prayer circles or meditative gatherings, that center on empowerment and renewal.
Key Practice: Encourage self-care and community care as integral to sustained activism.

Practical Tools for Empowerment
Study Guides: Use feminist scripture commentaries, like "The Women's Bible Commentary," to deepen understanding of reinterpreted texts.
Workshops: Host events that teach participants how to use scripture as a resource for personal and collective liberation.
Digital Platforms: Share resources and reinterpreted passages online to reach a broader audience and inspire global solidarity.

Advocacy and Policy Engagement
Strategy: Link scriptural principles with calls for systemic change.
*Example*: Advocate for policies that promote gender equity, citing biblical themes of justice and inclusion.
Application: Engage with local, national, and international platforms to amplify the moral imperative for social justice.
Key Practice: Use scripture-based advocacy materials in lobbying efforts, petitions, and public forums.

# About EATMS Productions

What's happening to women now is not random. It's structural.

Policy, culture, technology, and power are moving in the same direction.

EATMS maps them clearly and shows how to respond.

This title is part of an ongoing body of work. All EATMS Productions titles, across all series, authors, and formats, are components of a single connected project.

Start here: EATMS System Primer — Free Bundle
https://eatms.gumroad.com/l/dyvzbw

For full catalog or inquiries: eatms.me

Free survival booklet + EATMS updates: email "EATMS" to eatms@pm.me

*Please feel free to burn part or all of this book, safely, as an effigy.*